*Thank You, America*

Best wishes to
Long Time Friends
Dorothy and Sonny Rose

Buddy Bergman

BENJAMIN N. BERGER

# Thank You, America

THE BIOGRAPHY of BENJAMIN N. BERGER

by Robert K. Krishef

DILLON PRESS, INC., 500 SOUTH 3RD STREET, MINNEAPOLIS, MN

© 1982 by Benjamin N. Berger. All rights reserved.

Library of Congress Cataloging in Publication Data

Krishef, Robert K.
 Thank you, America.

1. Berger, Benjamin N. 2. Philanthropists—United States—Biography. I. Title.
HV28.B47K74  1982       361.7'4'0924 [B]       82-9733
ISBN 0-87518-236-4

*"There's nothing I wouldn't do for America."*
— Benjamin N. Berger

# Introduction

What if Benjamin N. Berger had not struck off on his own at the young-old age of sixteen, emigrating from Poland to the United States of America in 1913?

Would someone else have sent his brothers money and given them the courage to leave also? Or would they have followed their mother and father and sisters and brothers-in-law into the ovens of Treblinka?

Would another small-town theater owner have fought the battle against the Paramounts, Columbias, MGMs, and other giant movie studios of the thirties and forties?

Would someone else have founded the Minneapolis Lakers, the champion professional basketball team that was the forerunner of the Los Angeles Lakers?

Would someone else have risked personal bankruptcy to sue ASCAP, the omnipotent American Society of Composers, Authors, and Publishers?

Would some other layman have been able to peel back the bureaucratic layers and effect prison reform in Minnesota, giving hope of parole to hundreds of prisoners on life sentences?

Would someone else have risked the wrath of the Ku Klux Klan in Hallock, Minnesota?

Would the invisible discrimination barrier against Jews in Minneapolis service clubs have been as effectively pierced as it was by this self-taught, self-made, self-motivated Jewish immigrant from Poland?

Would another philanthropist have publicly supported abortions by donating $225,000 to the Planned Parenthood Clinic, despite violent resentment against the clinic in some circles?

Would another person have funded extensive research into the causes of crime in America?

Would there have been someone else dedicated and capable enough to raise such large amounts of money for Israel, for the Variety Club Heart Hospital at the University of Minnesota, and for other causes so germane to the human conscience?

Nobody is indispensable, they say. So, if there had been no Ben Berger, American, perhaps his role would have been filled and the deeds accomplished by someone else.

Perhaps.

## Chapter One

If there were a Speechmakers Hall of Fame, chances are that Ben Berger would be in it. Berger has been described as a person who "will accept a speaking invitation at the drop of a hat." A second characterization goes a bit further: "And he'll start talking before the hat hits the floor."

The description exaggerates. But not by much. Berger has addressed possibly a larger variety of audiences more times on more subjects than anyone else in the Upper Midwest, if not in the entire country. Over two hundred organizations and clubs have heard him speak, including Kiwanis, Lions, Elks, Optimist, American Legion, Veterans of Foreign Wars, Jewish National Fund, B'nai B'rith, Zionist Organization of America, Histadrut, Independent Theater Owners, Minnesota Prisoners Aid Society, National Conference of Christians and Jews—the list goes on and on; it resembles the roster of organizations in the Minneapolis yellow pages.

Curiously enough, about the only time Berger ever resisted the temptation to make speeches was when he ran for public office—for Commissioner of the Minneapolis Park Board—in 1963. By that time, he was already a well-known businessman, sports magnate, and philanthropist. He figured, and apparently correctly so, since he was elected and then reelected for a second six-year term in 1969, that his name was politically influential enough. Besides, Berger did not pretend to be an expert on the subject of parks. "What the hell did I know about trees?" he was to say years later.

This, however, was not an admission of inability to serve effectively. Rather, it was an expression of confidence in what might be termed the "Berger code of conduct," which maintains that even if you don't know how deep the water is, you can still jump in—as long as you know how to get help before you start to sink. What Berger has always had is the ability to ferret out information when he required it and to understand how to use the information when he had it. Thus, if he was not familiar with trees, that would not prevent him from learning how to shake, rattle, and sway them; or, to put it another way, he could learn how to become an influential park board commissioner. Which he did.

"I've been involved in a lot of things," he says, "and I haven't been trained in any of them. But I have common sense, and I know where to go to get advice. I can listen to both sides and make an intelligent decision, and when I get involved, I'm a good juror."

\* \* \*

One of Berger's most historic forays into, for him, uncharted waters came in 1944. He and Al Steffes, a partner in some movie theater ventures, bought Schiek's Cafe, the oldest restaurant in Minneapolis.

Fred Schiek served the first order of sauerbraten and potato pancakes in his new cafe on Washington Avenue in

1862. That was only six years after the city itself was founded. Washington Avenue was then the principal street, but gradually the street lost its prestigious image. So in 1887 Schiek moved his restaurant to a plush new location next door to an opera house on South Third Street, where patrons dined amidst the splendor of tall wall mirrors, handsome mahogany paneling, and paintings of chaste nudes on the ceiling. He added to the decor by paying the extravagant sum of $25,000 for a 100-foot-long mahogany bar from the 1904 St. Louis World's Fair.

The bar was installed in 1906, the year that Fred Schiek died. His son, Louis, took over the restaurant and operated it in the same tradition as his father, but with some definite thoughts about fine German dining. One of them was that beer and strawberries were incompatible and should never be eaten at the same meal. He could hardly conceal his consternation one day when a customer drank a mug of Schiek's tasty dark beer and then immediately consumed a strawberry shortcake with no harm to the digestive system.

Louis also had a promotional bent. Behind the bar was a ceramic boot that held at least two gallons of beer. He offered to fill the boot free for anyone who could drain it on the spot. There is no record of a successful contender, although some hardy souls of the era surely must have tried.

Louis Schiek died in 1943, by which time the restaurant's glorious reputation had become somewhat tarnished. The business was losing money, and Schiek's widow immediately started looking for a buyer. Enter Steffes and Berger.

"How about it, Bennie?" asked Steffes, who used to be a bartender at Schiek's. "Do you want to buy the place with me?"

"Come on, Al," Berger replied to the big, red-faced Steffes. "You're a German Catholic and I'm a Polish Jew. Only Greeks and Chinese can run a restaurant successfully. What do we know about it?"

Even while he was joking, however, Berger's fertile mind was analyzing the offer and appraising the possibilities. He saw a business that admittedly was run down, but that still had the nucleus of a veteran staff (some employees had been working there for fifty years), a built-in clientele, and at least the remnants of a good reputation. All that was needed, he decided, was application of common sense in order to clean up the situation—literally, because there were bugs scampering around the kitchen floor.

He went back to Steffes. "Okay, Al," he agreed, "I see no reason why we can't make Schiek's a first-class spot again."

Since buyers had not exactly been beating down the door, civic-minded citizens breathed a collective sigh of relief when Steffes and Berger bought the restaurant and preserved an institution. Some years later, Berger, who acquired Steffes' interest in 1946, found out how much of an institution his business really was. While installing a new boiler and cooling system in the basement, he discovered a potpourri of memorabilia hidden away in long-forgotten, dungeonlike compartments under the sidewalk.

There was wine and liquor dating back to Fred Schiek's day, photographs, delicate glassware, and original artwork, including a drawing of Sarah Bernhardt by Toulouse-Lautrec and a caricature of himself by Enrico Caruso. Registration books contained clippings about famous guests, and handwritten entries of note, such as "Bar closed, June 30, 1919" and "Beer back, April 7, 1933"—the start and finish of the Prohibition era.

All of this was fascinating to Berger, an inveterate history buff. But customers weren't about to patronize the restaurant out of civic pride or a sense of tradition. Schiek's was more or less drifting along until 1949, when Berger "got an idea," to use one of his familiar expressions. It was while listening to a Monday night radio program, "The Railroad Hour," which featured songs from Broadway musicals. Bells began to ring in Berger's show business-inclined mind, which had developed from years spent as a promoter for vaudeville, burlesque, stock companies, road shows, and concerts. What if, he thought, Schiek's formed a group of young people, say, three fellows and three girls, to perform "minishows"—forty or forty-five minutes of songs from Broadway musicals and light operettas? Wouldn't such wholesome and different live family entertainment, plus good food and service, be an irresistible magnet? Wouldn't it draw the crowds?

Berger concluded that it would. He hired a theatrical producer, Glyde Snyder, to find fresh new faces. He wanted talented amateurs, preferably University of Minnesota students, rather than professionals. "Kids would be more attractive to our customers," he told Snyder. "Besides," his eyes twinkled, "they won't cost me as much money."

That's how the Schiek's Sextette was born. An idea since copied by many other nightclubs, the Sextette was an immediate hit, doing six or seven encores a show. "I had to stop that and limit them to two or three encores," Berger recalls. "Otherwise we would have been playing practically the whole show over again." Almost overnight, the restaurant became the in spot of the Twin Cities, starting a new tradition, and a profitable one, even though it defied the normal nightclub ratio of fifty to seventy-five percent of business done at the bar. Only about thirty to thirty-five percent of Schiek's volume was in liquor. "We were a family place," says Berger. "We never even needed a bouncer."

The Sextette, he says, was his only real contribution to the success of Schiek's. "I didn't know anything about the restaurant business when I got into it, and I knew exactly the same when I got out twenty-seven years later."

\* \* \*

If this is true, it is difficult to equate with the image of Ben Berger as a dominant and confident personality. One can hardly imagine him spending twenty-seven years in any business without having more than a passing familiarity with the object of his investment, even if he does leave day-to-day management to others.

Berger has always been an intense and intelligent student, without ever having spent a day in an American school or, since the age of fourteen, in any other school. When something interests him, he studies it with the riveted attention of a would-be lawyer cramming for the bar exam. As a boy in his native Poland, Berger was a voracious reader. After his arrival in the United States, he read, as well as listened, in order to teach himself English. When he was seventeen, he worked as a vendor on the Minneapolis and St. Louis Railroad route between Minneapolis and Chicago. During the day, he walked the aisles. During the night, he studied the newspapers and magazines he was selling and read other material people left behind.

Later, while Berger was in the army awaiting assignment in a camp outside of Le Havre, France, an order came from the censor's office in Paris. The office needed twelve soldiers who were reasonably competent in a foreign language. Berger was among those picked. He figured, logically enough, that he was selected because of his ability to read and write Polish, Russian, and Yiddish. Instead, in its mysterious wisdom, the army took the young man who was still struggling to improve his English and put him to work censoring the letters that American soldiers were writing home.

Berger didn't complain. "I was one happy soldier," he says. He made the rank of corporal, which paid him forty-six dollars a month. He earned additional income by selling cigarettes (he didn't smoke), which many organizations gave away free to soldiers. He got to Monte Carlo on leave, and in Paris in the evenings, he was free to come and go as he chose. Each evening after dinner, he walked to Place de Bastille and to the Jewish area of the city, the Rue de Rivoli. "The only way I knew I was in the army," he says, "is that I wore a uniform, and each day we were marched three blocks to a public park for calisthenics."

Most of all, however, he appreciated his assignment. The benefit to the military was questionable. But for Berger, the experience of censoring 150 letters a day for nine months enhanced his English considerably.

Through the years there were still times when the student stumbled over his choice of words. In New York once, Berger and his wife, Midge, were taken out to dinner by a member of a copyright law firm and his wife. They were wined and dined in glorious fashion and when the evening was over, Berger thanked his hosts effusively: "When you come to Minneapolis, Joe, I want you and Jean to be guests of Midge and myself. You have treated us so wonderfully that I want to retaliate."

By and large, however, Berger took command of the English language like General Patton over his troops. His verbalizing reflected an intrinsic fire-eating nature, and his confrontations with movie studio executives became legends in their own time.

At a meeting in Los Angeles in 1949, producer Stanley Kramer told independent theater owners that screen credits—listings of the set designers, makeup artists, sound technicians, writers, and anyone who had a hand in the development of a motion picture—would be getting longer and longer. The theater owners objected, knowing that if credits became too long, pictures could not be shown as many times during the day, which would reduce theater revenue.

Kramer, however, was unsympathetic. "There's nothing you can do about it," he shrugged.

Berger stood, bristling. "I want to tell you, Mr. Kramer, that we are going to have the last word," he fired back. "You make those credits longer and we are going to make them shorter by snip, snip, snipping them right off onto the booth floor."

Anger is not the only emotion that brings out Berger's penchant for debating, arguing, or turning a phrase in his adopted language. The *Minneapolis Star* some years ago asked prominent local citizens to write epitaphs about themselves. What would they like people to say and know about them after they died? Most of the replies were humorous or frivolous.

Criminal attorney Ronald Meshbesher responded with succinct wit, "The defense rests."

One of Minnesota's best-known congressmen, and now mayor of Minneapolis, Donald Fraser, wrote, "Here, Donald Fraser, politician, lies for the first time."

Dave Moore, a newscaster for WCCO Television, suggested for his tombstone, "He fled from the dread of the news he read."

Berger's answer, though, was deeply serious and emotional. He never passed up a chance to say thanks to America. "I am singularly fortunate," he wrote, "given the opportunity to move from the uncovered wagon to the fulfillment of the great American dream, thankfully earning community respect."

\* \* \*

But it is speaking to a crowd that, more than anything else, stirs Berger's juices like those of an actor when the cameras begin to roll. During one speech, he got so wound up that the wife of his attorney thought he was going to have a heart attack on the spot. "Don't worry, honey," advised the attorney, Sid Feinberg, who had witnessed Berger's speeches before. "Ben always gives a speech this way."

Berger never writes a speech beforehand—"that's because you can't read your own handwriting," Midge Berger will quip irreverently. He talks spontaneously for perhaps thirty to forty-five minutes, with some kind of internal alarm clock enabling him to package his address into the allotted time coherently. It's sort of a talk-as-you-go plan, and seldom does he overstep his time by more than three or four minutes. He is far from a polished, professional orator. But most listeners agree that he is effective because of his knowledge of his subject, remarkable enthusiasm, and obvious sincerity. One Minneapolis American Legion Post has heard him speak three different times.

"People have to be impressed because Ben is so genuine," says District Court Judge Neil Riley. "There isn't a phony bone in his entire body."

Riley, who is intimately familiar with Berger's compassion and concern for people, has those qualities himself. He is the kind of judge who doesn't allow his elevated position on the bench to keep him from being down to earth, an attitude revealed by the story he tells of the day his mother, a hard-working soul, came into his courtroom for the first time. "Is that all my son does?" she finally remarked. "I never had an easy day like that in all my life."

The kindred spirits, Berger and Riley, played key roles in founding the Minnesota organization Amicus, which is Latin for friend. Amicus was formed to provide one-to-one relationships for former prisoners during the critical adjustment period following their release from prison. In 1967, using volunteers to help reduce the apalling rate of recidivism among past offenders was a new idea. Berger had already taken an active role in prison reform and in aiding ex-convicts financially; so when Riley's new organization needed start-up money, he went to Berger for help.

"It was the first time that I had met Ben," says Riley. He told me about his previous work and I told him what my aspirations were for Amicus."

Berger admired the aspirations but was cautious about the other man's depth of commitment. "Is this idea just a passing fancy or are you going to stick with it?" he demanded. "I don't intend to be associated with a failure."

"Neither do I," answered Riley.

"Well, how much do you want?"

Riley hesitated. He was on unfamiliar turf in more ways than one. He was having lunch at Schiek's. The owner—Berger—was picking up the tab. And he—Riley—didn't know what to ask for. In fact, he had never known how to raise money. He took a deep breath. "How about $5,000?"

"No," said Ben flatly.

The judge's heart sank momentarily, but he had expected a no and was willing to take anything he could get. He was quickly mulling over a counter-suggestion when Berger continued.

"No, $5,000 isn't enough. It will take a minimum of $7,000."

Before the year was out, Berger had donated $9,000 to float the new organization, and in ensuing years he contributed $100,000 more.

He threw himself into leadership of Amicus with his accustomed fervor, becoming president of the organization. Many memorable moments followed, one of which came in 1974, at the annual Amicus dinner. The guest speaker was Elliott Richardson, former attorney general of the United States; he had resigned that post the previous year rather than obey President Nixon's order to fire Watergate prosecutor, Archibald Cox. After Richardson's talk, Judge Riley unexpectedly strode to the podium.

"I have an announcement," he began. "Unknown to Ben Berger, we have chosen this occasion to pay tribute to him for his inspiration to Amicus, the friend of the downtrodden." Richardson, he added, would present a special plaque.

Berger accepted in a state of shock. The prearranged ceremony had caught him completely unprepared. For one of the few times in his life, he was absolutely speechless. He took the only possible course in what was for him an unusual predicament. He bit the bullet and admitted that he didn't know what to say. But the confession was premature, for suddenly he remembered an event that he had attended long before. His feelings then, he realized, were appropriate to this occasion as well. The words started flowing like a gusher as Ben Berger, reverting to form, told the story of another day.

# Chapter Two

*I was invited to a White House luncheon given in 1954 by President Eisenhower. There were thirty-six guests. The room was set up with six tables, six people at each table, except for the head table where the president also sat. Seating was fixed ahead of time, of course—everything was according to the strictest protocol—and I was put at the head table. I don't know why. I'm not even sure why I was considered important enough to be invited in the first place, and so to be at the head table was really something.*

*True, Eisenhower knew about my work. I had raised quite a bit of money for Korean War relief. And for three years I was state chairman of the Crusade for Freedom, which raised funds to support Radio Free Europe. A year or so earlier, the government had sent me to Europe with a delegation to visit some of the radio transmitter sites from which news was broadcast behind the Iron Curtain.*

*I had also represented the United States government at the first Berlin Film Festival, along with Bob Hope, Eric Johnston, and some others. Little things about that trip* stick in my mind. When I was in the army in Europe in 1918, I was just a corporal. This time, a general gave me a ride back to my hotel. It's sort of silly, I guess, but having a general offer me a ride gave me a thrill.

We saw a number of films at the festival. One of them was a short subject from Russia, a two-reeler that was only about twenty minutes long. The color and photography were outstanding. American filmmakers didn't spend the kind of money it must have taken to produce that short subject. The Russian producer was there, and Bob Hope and I were among the Americans talking to him. We asked him what his budget had been in order to make such a terrific film. He answered, in all seriousness, "What's a budget?" In other words, he had no budget. He didn't have to worry about what it cost. All he had to worry about was making it good, which I guess was something to worry about, too.

Eisenhower also knew me from politics. I had been an active Republican most of my life. One time Daniel Gainey, the Republican state chairman in Minnesota, invited me to a fundraising meeting at the Minneapolis Club, a place for real bluebloods. Gainey wanted me to give a little speech. Politics makes strange bedfellows. "You know, I'm a Jew," I told those at the meeting. "If it weren't for politics, I wouldn't have been able to walk in the front door of this building." They all laughed. They got a real kick out of that remark. I think.

Eisenhower, by the way, wasn't the Republican I had been working for originally—Harold Stassen was the man. This was when Stassen was a credible candidate. His running for president finally got to be a joke. But don't kid yourself about Stassen. He's no dummy. Running for president has given him a forum for being in front of the public and expressing his views. He couldn't buy that kind of publicity.

But anyway, whatever the reasons, here I was at the White House. One of the people at the head table with me was David Rockefeller. I talked to him a bit, and I also chatted with the man next to me, a tall, personable fellow, in his early fifties, I supposed. His name was Alexander—we all had place cards—Henry Clay Alexander. He said he was originally from Tennessee. When he learned that I was from Minneapolis, he said, "Well, I have one acquaintance there I know pretty well. Joe Ringland. Say hello to him for me when you get back."

"Oh sure," I said. "I will. I know Joe. He's my state treasurer in Crusade for Freedom. He's head of Northwest Banco. Are you in the banking business, too?"

"Yes," Alexander said. "I'm president of J. P. Morgan."

Well, I'm sure I must have continued talking after that. But I don't remember any of the conversation. All I remember is thinking that I came to this country at the age of sixteen, unable to speak a word of English, and now, here I was at the White House, sitting with the president of the United States. With me at the same table was a Rockefeller, who came from a family so wealthy that it made me seem like a pauper. Next to me was the president of J. P. Morgan, and I was having a personal conversation with him. To me, all of this was fantastic. My thoughts might sound corny to some, but I meant them then, I mean them now, and I will mean them as long as I live. Where else but in America could this have happened to a Jewish immigrant from Ostrowiec, Poland?

## Chapter Three

In the tortured history of Poland, the town of Ostrowiec is barely worthy of a footnote. It is but one of scores of communities on or near the banks of the country's primary river, the Vistula, which wends its way northward from the interior and empties into the Gulf of Danzig on the Baltic Sea.

When Beryl Nachum Berger was born March 5, 1897, Ostrowiec had a population of approximately ten thousand—of whom about sixty-one hundred were Jewish. In the early 1920s, the general population had risen to twenty thousand and the number of Jews had reached a high of around ten thousand one hundred. In the 1930s, the Jewish population began to drop; there were about eight thousand Jews in Ostrowiec when Nazi Germany attacked Poland on September 1, 1939.

The trickle of Jewish emigration from Ostrowiec, so tragically late and slow, started when a few people began to see the bloody handwriting on the wall. There was, to be sure, the impending threat of Hitler, but another reason for concern and despair was the increasingly vicious anti-Semitism in Poland. This chilling trend intruded like a nightmare on the occasion that had brought Ben and Midge Berger to Poland in April 1937.

They had been married about eighteen months—the first marriage for her, the second for Ben; his first marriage, in 1923, had ended in divorce in 1934. Midge had never met her in-laws, so she was looking forward to this trip. The visit also was timed so that they would observe Passover, the Jewish holiday celebrating the exodus from Egypt, with Ben's family.

There was a slight problem in introducing the new Mrs. Berger. "Ben's parents thought I was a 'shiksa' because I couldn't speak Yiddish," says Midge. "Fortunately, while we were there a letter arrived for them from my father. It said that he and my mother would miss us at the Passover *seder* in St. Paul, but that they were happy to share us with Ben's parents in Poland. And the letter was written in Yiddish! That convinced my in-laws that I was Jewish."

Under normal circumstances, the seder would have been a blessed experience. Passover, with its enduring messages of hope, of struggle, of freedom, and of thankfulness, is an emotional period for Jews. With the added presence of a son and his new wife from America, everyone should have been bathed in joy—except that circumstances in Poland were far from normal. Fear and uncertainty permeated the atmosphere.

Later, when he and Midge were in their room at the Hotel Europejski in Warsaw, Ben sat in stony, reflective silence. He had begun the habit of recording his thoughts and observations while on trips. Now, he angrily wrote, "I am unable to find polite words to describe the Polish attitude toward Jews. Animals are being treated more humanely than the Jewish population."

The proof was all around them. It was found in daily reports of Jews being beaten and sent to hospitals with cuts inflicted by specially designed sticks or canes, which had razor blades inserted in the tip. There were almost daily occurrences of vandals breaking up tombstones in Jewish cemeteries. "It seems to be the national sport," wrote Berger bitterly. Jews were being sent to jail for supposedly making derogatory remarks about public officials. There were government-sponsored boycotts of Jewish stores, and restrictions against Jews practicing law, medicine, or other such prestigious professions. "The Jews in Poland today are like a man tied to a post and being whipped to death," Berger wrote.

It was an almost prophetic comment, made even more painfully poignant because of the holiday during which it was expressed. Passover stood for the moment in history when Moses gathered his flock and escaped from slavery. Ben wished that his father would gather his flock—his family—and escape, too. But the decision was not that simple for Chaim Berger, nor for his counterparts throughout Europe. They were living in bad times, true, but they had always been living in bad times. They were used to it, as much as people could get used to it, and they hoped that things would get better—they didn't want to believe that things could get worse.

The elder Berger listened to his son, Beryl (who had somehow become "Benjamin" or "Bennie" in America but was still "Beryl" in Poland) trying to persuade him to leave. "But what will I do in America?" he responded. "I'm not ready to just go to *schul*. Here, everybody knows me. The sidewalks know me. I was born here. My father was born here. My grandfather was born here." He spoke halfway between a sigh and a shrug. "I don't want to go unless I can be active in something."

By February 1939, Chaim Berger had changed his mind. Ben received a letter in which his father stated, "Things are getting rough. We have decided that we want to come to America." For him to have admitted such readiness was tantamount to a silent shriek. The desperate plight leaped from between the lines like invisible ink coming to life. Ben acted swiftly, but has carried the burden ever since that he wasn't fast enough. He tells the story stolidly, as if drained by the effort.

"I made application immediately and my parents heard from the American Embassy in Warsaw in April or May. Then they wrote that they had been to the embassy and that everything was all right. They would be getting their visas."

Shortly after that, however, Berger received an inquiry from Washington, asking if his father had been to the United States before. This question had evidently been prompted by something that had been said, or something that someone thought had been said, during the interview at the embassy in Warsaw. In any event, it slowed the ponderous wheels of bureaucracy even more. The delay might have been the fatal stroke, or perhaps the Berger family would not have had time to leave, regardless. No one will ever know. But, Ben Berger thinks about it, and wonders.

"I should never have answered that inquiry by mail," he says. "I should have gotten some lawyer on the telephone to Washington right away. But who the hell figured that war was going to start in September?" He paused, and then added quietly, "I should have been able to get them out."

Ben was frustrated by the memory of the 1937 conversation with his father. Their discussion, after all, had not been merely an academic exercise, but rather had had life-or-death implications. Ben was proud of his accomplishments in the new land and confident about his intellectual prowess and ability to persuade. He was a man not used to failure. But he had been unable to convince his own father to change his mind before it was too late.

Yet another part of him understood Chaim Berger's reasoning. Ben could empathize with his father. He knew how the elder Berger felt and realized why he had clung to chaos and resisted for so long the unknown consequences of being uprooted.

In the midst of chaos, at least Chaim Berger had his own identity. He was struggling to preserve his individuality; in that sense, he was very much like Poland itself.

\* \* \*

Although Poland is some eight hundred years older than the United States, it endured a history of traumatic subservience over roughly the same period in which America emerged as a nation. Poland was partitioned in 1772 by Russia, Prussia, and Austria, and further subdivided in 1793 by Russia and Prussia. It finally ceased to exist as a separate nation in 1795, when it was partitioned once more by Russia, Prussia, and Austria.

In 1830 and again in 1863, the Poles revolted against Russian rule, Russia being in control of the vast majority of Polish soil. Defeated both times, the Polish people continued to chafe at their status and yearn for their independence, which they ultimately won following the end of World War I in 1918. Boundaries of the new Polish Republic encompassed territory that three different countries had ripped away nearly one hundred fifty years before. But the end of the war "to end all wars" did not mark the beginning of a contented Poland.

There were continuing clashes between Poland and Russia and between Poland and Germany (nee Prussia).

Huge pockets of poverty dotted the nation. The government was unstable and the political process was further aggravated by inner strife between rightists and Bolsheviks. For nearly one hundred fifty years, Poland had been dependent, disillusioned, restless. Now she was free, disillusioned, restless—and ripe for a scapegoat.

Jews had been living in Poland since the birth of the country, but mass immigration did not begin until around the twelfth century. The immigrant flow was eastward principally, from German and Bohemian lands. Jews sought to escape from fanatical persecution during the Crusades and from preposterous accusations, such as being charged with "responsibility" for epidemics such as the Black Death. Poland was viewed by many new immigrants as a refuge, perhaps reflecting the desperate human need to have hope, whether justified by the facts or not. There *were* occasional intervals of relative tranquility for the Jewish people in Poland, but the gradual disintegration of the country's fabric, plus the continuing fears born of ignorance and accentuated by religious differences, inevitably increased the momentum of misery heaped on Jews. The myths of prejudice were not dissolved at the sight of Jews fighting alongside their fellow Poles—and Jews did consider Poland their homeland—in uprisings in the 1790s, in 1830, in 1863, and in the battles that finally led to liberation in 1918.

This was the difficult world before and during the lifetime of Chaim Berger. If it wasn't a world that he loved, it was one that he accepted as his lot in life, the only one he knew until he was killed in the Holocaust. In 1892 he married a sweet, determined young lady named Roza Kalechman. It was a foregone conclusion that they would settle in their home village of Ostrowiec. Members of their generation rarely were provided with the vision or the means to chase elusive dreams elsewhere. They looked for ways to find the strength to live, to instill a sense of tradition in the next generation, and to deal with whatever exigencies God scattered in their path, and they drew strength from their *shtetl* as well as from their souls.

\* \* \*

*Shtetl* was the term for a distinctively and exclusively Jewish settlement occupying a specific area of a town or village. The *shtetl* arose out of the instinctive need of people to draw together during threatening moments—which meant all the time for the Jews of Eastern Europe. In addition, however, the *shtetl* was an offshoot of policies that, throughout the centuries, frequently restricted the Jews to certain sections of a town.

In Poland, for example, a governing authority, called the Council of the Four Lands, supervised and regulated the activities and movements of Jewish communities for nearly two hundred years, until the latter third of the eighteenth century. Rabbis participated in council assemblies—in 1755, the Rabbi of Ostrowiec, Ezekiel B. Avigdor, was among the representatives. But it can be safely assumed that the role of Jewish members was to convey decisions back to their respective congregations, rather than to participate in discussions.

Jewish communities varied both in size and in socioeconomic viability. Unfortunately, Ostrowiec ranked at the low end of the scale, even for a *shtetl*, when Chaim and Roza Berger were raising their family. When Ben Berger talks about it, he sounds almost as if he is doing a parody on "we were so poor jokes," except that he isn't laughing; he is using the conditions from which he sprang as a counterpoint in explaining his gratitude to the United States of America. "In our town," he says, "if you weren't wearing clothes with patches, you were considered rich."

In retrospect, there is often a tendency to wax nostalgic and glorify the memories and experiences of childhood. Not so with Berger. "I was never really a kid," he remarks. "We never had toys or birthday parties. If we got a present, it was usually an orange or something like that." There were, of course, no organized games or activities for children. Berger recalls gathering, at the age of five or six, with other youngsters in a *podwosh*—a fenced-in area in back of a house—where they pretended they were soldiers. He also found ways to amuse himself when he was alone. A favorite pastime was to climb through a skylight type of window leading to the roof of his house, where he would build shelters for birds to land and feed on bread crumbs. "Why I never fell off that roof and broke my neck I'll never know," he muses.

The Berger house incorporated only the barest necessities. That did not include toilet paper. "We used newspapers or tore up paper bags," says Berger. Naturally there was no electricity or running water; a weekly ritual every Friday was a shower at the community bathhouse. There were two rooms to the Berger house. In the daytime, one bed was converted into a table. Four children slept in another bed, two at each end. Eventually there were seven children in all—the last one was born after Ben left for the United States.

The only plentiful food in the household was bread and potatoes. There was no butter and little milk; a glass of milk actually consisted of one-third milk and two-thirds hot water. Berger's midday meal usually was two pieces of dark bread, which he took to school with him. "We never had a first-class meal," he relates, "except for the *Shabbat* Friday evening and for holidays." For these special occasions, dinner usually consisted of chicken or pea soup; gefilte fish, an oblong-shaped meatballish blend of chopped fish and bread crumbs; chicken as the main course; and for dessert, *tsimmes*, which was a mixture of dried fruit.

Yet, compared with the deprivation others suffered, the Bergers were reasonably well off. Chaim Berger on occasion was worth as much as two thousand to three thousand rubles, the equivalent of one thousand to fifteen hundred dollars. "That was a lot more than many other Jewish families in our town had," says Ben.

Chaim's "worth" was based on modest savings and on his humble property and inventory. He was a merchant of sorts, a middleman providing a conduit for distribution of goods, buying from one party at the lowest possible price and selling to another at the highest. Decades later, in the United States, Ben Berger would be a millionaire based on holdings of theaters, real estate, a restaurant, sports teams, and other investments, which he sometimes bought and sold much as his father had bought and sold chickens, fish, and geese.

Two days a week, Chaim dealt with farmers who came to Ostrowiec. Two other days, he journeyed to markets in outlying communities. He made these trips with his wagon—this was the "uncovered wagon" that Ben would later refer to in his "epitaph" in the *Minneapolis Star*.

The magnitude of Chaim Berger's trading was limited only by his imagination and confidence—which is to say that it was practically limitless. He believed that he could make a deal for anything somewhere, somehow. One time he committed himself to acquiring an entire railroad carload of geese, which he managed to wholesale off to some German buyers. On less profitable days, his scope of commerce shrank to wheeling and dealing for a half-dozen chickens, selling to women and waiting until they resold the chickens before he got his money.

Chaim was not familiar with the exact concept of "accounts receivable," but he did know that the money owed him caused his financial position to fluctuate wildly from time to time. He and all of the other merchants, producers, distributors, retailers, and consumers—many of whom occupied several roles simultaneously—were in the same leaky economic boat. Chaim was hardly influential enough to be considered the captain of the boat. But in the vocational caste system of the era, his profession was accorded reasonable respect, much more so than that of a gravedigger, for instance, or a chimney sweep.

"My father couldn't read or write, but he was a smart man," states Ben. "He had partners in various towns. Every Saturday night, they got together for an accounting. My father never had trouble figuring out what he had coming."

Still, what he had coming at any given time was hardly more than enough to keep the family plight from being entirely hopeless. Every week, every day, was a struggle. "We were living from hand to mouth," says Ben. "When my little sister was up crying all night with a terrible headache, we didn't even have an aspirin for her. I can understand the feelings of the 'have-nots' today, because I've been there."

The tableau he paints is remarkably familiar to present-day sociologists and social workers. The father was away from home much of the time, preoccupied with work, anxiously striving to earn a living for a growing young family. The mother also held a job—for many years Roza Berger sold bagels and other baked goods from her stand in the marketplace in the middle of town. The children were mostly on their own, taking care of themselves, knowing that if they wanted something special, such as a new pair of shoes, they had to find a way to earn their own money to pay for it.

Roza was the stabilizing influence in the household. She was the typical mother, Jewish and otherwise, of that generation, holding the family together, imparting traditional values, making decisions (although ensuring that Chaim Berger had final authority), washing, cleaning, cooking, and applying proper measures of discipline. If for Jews the *shtetl* was the planet around which Poland revolved, then the home was the body around which the *shtetl* revolved. From this core came a wellspring of strength.

There must have been moments of discouragement for Roza Berger. After a particularly trying day of meeting the responsibilities of the outer world as well as those of her household, sporadic doubts may have flickered through her mind like the flame from the kerosene lamp beside her.

Chaim Berger assumed that his sons would follow in his footsteps and do what he was doing, just as he had followed in the footsteps of his father, and his father in the footsteps of *his* father, all in the town of Ostrowiec. But maybe Roza now and then stopped to ask herself if there wasn't more to life. Maybe it was from her that one of her sons, Beryl, inherited the spirit and the urge to find something better.

# Chapter Four

You could have knocked Chaim Berger over with a goose down feather from the mattress of a rich family's dowry when his son, Beryl, made his stunning announcement in 1911. "Papa, I want to go to live and work in Warsaw." After all, the boy was only fourteen, a rather tender age for him to be "schlepping" off alone to the big city, which was some one hundred fifty kilometers north, in practically another universe. It was true that, at fourteen, a year after his *bar mitzvah*, he was considered for all intents and purposes full grown and capable of starting to meet adult responsibilities. But to leave home at that age was another matter. Besides, if he could meet adult responsibilities there was a compelling reason for keeping him at home, where he could contribute more effectively to the welfare of the family.

"Ridiculous!" snapped Chaim. "What do you want to go to Warsaw for?"

Beryl faced his father unflinchingly. They were alike in many ways. Short, but strongly built. Opinionated.

Confident. Although the boy respected Chaim, this was one instance in which he felt that he knew more than his father, and he wouldn't, he just couldn't, give in. He tried to explain the frustration and restlessness within him. "I have to go, Papa. I just can't stay here anymore. There's got to be a better life for me somewhere else." He paused, "Maybe it's in Warsaw."

Chaim Berger sighed. Sometimes he wished that his second oldest wasn't quite so self-reliant and independent. It reminded him of himself. "What's the matter with the life here?" he demanded. "Your older brother doesn't seem to mind it."

"I know he doesn't," nodded Beryl. That was a fact. Sam, who was two years older, *was* satisfied to go along with their father. "But I'm different. Please, Papa," he continued. "Let me go."

"Where will you live?"

"I'll stay with Aunt Malka."

Chaim shook his head. "My sister doesn't have room for you. She's got her own family to worry about."

"Then I'll find my own place to live."

The dialogue went on at some length and Chaim also discussed the matter with Roza. But his heart wasn't in it because he knew that the discussion was academic. There was just no way, short of chaining Beryl to a tree, that they were going to be able to prevent their young, headstrong son from seeking his destiny elsewhere. Moreover, Chaim realized that, although he might not want to admit it, in some respects Beryl indeed did know more than he. This was the boy who was referred to, not only in his own family, but throughout the *shtetl*, as "the educated one"— and for good reason.

Although education was a sublime goal in most Jewish homes, and all Jewish boys started learning to read

Yiddish and Hebrew in *cheder* when they were three or three and a half years old, not all of them absorbed instruction as quickly or had minds as sharply inquiring as did little Beryl Berger. Knowledge for him was a form of mental nourishment, which he gladly took in increasingly large doses as he grew, proceeding from the Hebrew alphabet to the study of the Bible and Jewish history and traditions.

His parents were not taxpayers, so Beryl could not enter public school. But recognizing his potential, they scraped together enough funds to enroll him in a private Polish school at the age of eight and a half. He was the only one of, at that time, four Berger children to enter such a school. There he learned Polish, arithmetic, and other fundamental skills. In addition, one day a week of his secular schooling was devoted to reading and writing Russian, since this part of Poland belonged to Russia, although not formally annexed by it.

His Polish education, which continued for five years, was far less intensive and personal, however, than was his Yiddish schooling. For about three hours after regular school, he and others his age would sit with their *melamed*, the teacher who instructed them and ultimately prepared them for *bar mitzvah*, in an atmosphere that today's educational purists would have loved. It was the basics, it was no-nonsense listening and learning, and it was practically one-to-one instruction, because a *melamed* often worked with only two or three youngsters at a time.

This fundamental type of upbringing was found in *shtetls* throughout Eastern Europe. Jews emerged from it with a certain kinship, whether they came from the region called Congress Poland, where Ostrowiec was located, or from the area immediately to the east. This eastern area, called the Pale of Jewish Settlement, was officially part of Russia.

Many years later, Beryl—now "Ben"—and his wife, Midge, were having lunch at the MGM Studios in Culver City, California. They were introduced to one of the most famous and feared of the Hollywood moguls, Louis B. Mayer, who had been born near Vilna in the Pale, asked the Bergers to his office for a chat. "There was no particular reason for him to invite us," says Ben. "I was prominent in the trade press, but we talked a lot more about the success Mayer was having breeding horses than we did about the movie business."

From the length of the informal conversation, which stretched from an expected few minutes into well over an hour, it was obvious that Mayer had taken a liking to the movie exhibitor "from somewhere back east in Minneapolis." Berger explains this simply by saying, "Well, we came out of the same kind of *cheder*," as if that clarified everything.

\* \* \*

Berger's formal schooling in Ostrowiec ended not long after he was bar mitzvahed, but his thirst for knowledge had hardly begun to be satiated, nor would it ever be. In the *shtetl*, even the poorest of Jewish homes had books, traditionally prayer books. In the Berger home, mostly because of the thirst of the "educated one," there were Yiddish history books, plus magazines and newspapers such as *der Moment* and *Haynt* in addition to the prayer books.

Much of the material was published in Warsaw, and this stimulated Ben's zeal to move to the big city. He figured that a place that spewed out so much information was a good point from which to start looking for a better world.

Although the world he found wasn't exactly better, it was infinitely more fascinating. There was so much more of everything in Warsaw than in Ostrowiec—Jews, Gentiles, horses, wagons, buildings, stores. If he was interested in an education, he got it, but in ways he didn't anticipate.

He was working in a wine store, washing and filling bottles and delivering them, the same kind of job he had back in Ostrowiec. About six months after his arrival, he went to a park one Saturday, which was his day off. A small crowd had gathered around a speaker. Berger idly joined the others, but before he even had a chance to hear what was being said, he was in the middle of a sudden maelstrom of police. The park, as it turned out, was a public nest of revolutionaries and malcontents.

"They marched the whole kaboodle of us off to the Pavia Street jail," says Berger. "I was there only about twenty-four hours. My employer got me out. Whenever someone didn't show up for work, jail was the first place they looked for you."

It was a bewildering, eye-opening, thought-provoking experience for a lad not quite fifteen, and there was much more to come. This was a turbulent era of transition; movements were afloat that spoke to the needs of the persecuted.

One of these movements was Zionism, the dream to create a homeland in Palestine for the Jewish people. The *shtetls* and *cheders* of Eastern Europe influenced different individuals in different ways. Louis B. Mayer's father, a Hebraic scholar, packed up his family and emigrated to Nova Scotia. David Ben-Gurion, on the other hand, left his home town of Plonsk at the age of twenty, moved to Palestine, and became an ardent Zionist, recruiter, and eventually, the first prime minister of the State of Israel. Ben-Gurion and his associates urged Jews to settle in Palestine, and they were seeking out just such prospects as young Berger.

Another movement, whose members believed in varying degrees of aggressive action, was socialism. Most

Jewish Socialists were part of an organization known as the Bund. They had a loose affiliation with other Poles and Russians who also wanted to overthrow the Czar—their common goal was a new form of government that would free people from enslavement and fear.

It was a goal Berger understood well. He remembered a playmate who had lost an eye, but whose family couldn't complain because the injury was inflicted by a Polish youth. He remembered being hit himself and having to walk away instead of retaliate, because he was a Jew.

Then there was the pogrom of 1905, when mobs roamed through the *shtetl* of Ostrowiec and of other Jewish communities in an unofficially sanctioned night of looting, burning, and sometimes killing. Eight-year-old Beryl huddled in the darkness with the rest of the Berger family, shaking to the sounds of shouting, cursing, taunting men trying to break down the heavily bolted and barred door. "They didn't get in, but they didn't care," says Ben. "That night they were really looking for shops and stores to destroy."

Such pogroms had been occurring in eastern Europe for more than 200 years. They had begun in Russia and, when one Czar after another made no effort to stop them, they spread to Russian captive countries such as Poland and Lithuania. Just before a pogrom, governments and public officials knew what was going to happen and when. Their troops, police, or Cossacks remained on the outskirts of the targeted Jewish settlements throughout the carnage, and moved in the next morning, after the despoilers had vanished, "to enforce the law and protect the people." It was a tidy arrangement.

* * *

Following the jailing incident in 1911, Berger's name went on some sort of list, which the revolutionary underground maintained with all of the intensity, if not the scientific computer precision, of today's direct mail specialists. He would appear to have been a promising, pliable candidate ripe for plucking, in view of his background, youthful age, and state of mind.

His state of mind was that he was bored. Although he was essentially independent and a bit of a loner, the endless string of evenings with nothing to do was becoming wearying. So when he got on the list to be notified of secret meetings in homes, he accepted the invitations as much out of relief as out of commitment. "They were looking for volunteers, for kids, whom they could break into the movement," he says. "I started attending two or three meetings a week, in a different home each night."

Occasionally Poles spoke at these meetings, but mostly the sessions were led by Jews, for Jews, while similar indoctrination was taking place in other homes for non-Jewish audiences. Perhaps if circumstances had thrown Berger into the company of another crowd, he would have been listening to Zionists night after night. Instead, his mentors probably were members of the Bund; he really didn't know. "I didn't know whether they were Socialists or Communists or what," he says. "But they were educated and spoke well, and they really did a selling job."

Their declarations about the existing system of government were issued like a series of jolting left jabs:

"People have no opportunities to get anywhere."

"The capitalists are bathing in gold while the rest of us are starving to death."

"We're living under autocratic rule."

"Kill the Czar!"

"The same thing must happen here as happened in the American Revolution."

Berger was not an easy person to mold, however, despite factors which, on the surface, might have indicated otherwise. He did not respond publicly to any of the comments; these meetings were not intended to be debating forums. Those invited were there to keep quiet and listen. But that didn't prevent Berger from debating within his own mind, as he absorbed the influx of information, however slanted or subjective, and measured it against the substantial knowledge he had been accumulating on his own.

"Yiddish history had made a hell of an impression on me," he says, "I used to cry sometimes when reading it, because nearly every page was saturated with innocent Jewish blood. This was wrong. This had to be changed. Then, when I was in Warsaw, I had a chance to read some newspaper stories about America. I read about Woodrow Wilson and the election of 1912. I learned about the American Constitution and realized that the people in America were really free."

The speakers' strategy backfired, as far as Ben Berger was concerned, when they urged those assembled to join them in revolution. They said the American Revolution was the torch that sparked the French Revolution, and that the same thing could happen in Russia and Poland. As they talked, Berger kept thinking about the American Constitution. About the right of a person to practice whatever religion he chose. About the fact that the police should have to get a warrant before going into someone's home to arrest him. About the general philosophy of human dignity and the right to pursuit of happiness.

The more they talked, the more they convinced Berger what his next step had to be.

# Chapter Five

*I went home and told my father that I wanted to go to America. You can imagine how that went over. If he hadn't wanted me to go from Ostrowiec to Warsaw, you can imagine how he felt about my going all the way to America.*

*Papa asked why I had to do this. I told him about the education I had received, what I had learned in Warsaw. "Kill the Czar" the revolutionaries had said. But I didn't want to kill the Czar or the capitalists or anyone else. I knew a lot about history. I saw what there was yesterday, I could see what we had today, and I believed that there could be something better tomorrow. I had to get away from a place where someone could decide to have a new law in the morning, pass it in the afternoon, and use it to throw you in jail in the evening.*

*I told my father that America was a free country. No one would beat me up. I would have rights, I could do what I wanted. I could find a job, then a better job. I could save some money, get somewhere, be someone.*

Neither of my parents was willing to let me go. It was natural. Parents didn't want to send their children off and perhaps never see them again. Mama hugged me. "Beryl, you're too young," she said. "You're only sixteen. What will you do? How will you live?"

Papa thought, too, that I could still be of value to him in Ostrowiec. And he was concerned about the cost. "How will you pay for the trip?" he asked.

That was a tough one. I didn't have any money. In Warsaw for two years, I had had a few different jobs. Working in a wine store, delivering, collecting bottles and sacking them. But you couldn't save much doing any of those things. I had spent most of my savings on the railroad ticket back home and on a new suit and shirt. When I had left home at fourteen, I was wearing patched clothes and had to hitch a ride to Warsaw on a hay wagon. I wanted to return to Ostrowiec in a decent way, looking nice. So I did. But that left me with only about thirty rubles—fifteen dollars.

It would cost my father 200 rubles to send me to America. That was just too much. He wouldn't let me go.

But I was determined. I didn't give my parents any alternative but to allow me to go to America. I refused to work in the business with my father, and I refused to cooperate around the house. I knew that this behavior wasn't right, but it was the only way I knew to convince them.

My parents talked some more. All I was at home was an extra mouth to feed. They loved me, but they could see that I was a lost sheep to them. My uncle—he was married to my mother's sister—had a sister living in Fargo, North Dakota, United States of America. His sister had sent tickets for him and his two daughters to come to Fargo. My father decided to let me travel with them—he gave me the 200 rubles.

*I left Poland late in the afternoon of August 10, 1913. My parents, two of my brothers, and my two sisters went to the railroad depot with me. My leaving was a hard time for all of us. Papa cried. It was the first time in my life that I had ever seen him cry. Mama cried, too, and that brought tears to my eyes as well.*

*Just before I got on board, Mama took my arm and stopped me. We were facing each other. She raised her hands above her, over my head, and "benched" me. She asked in this blessing that the good angel watch over me and take care of me for all time, wherever I went.*

*I'm superstitious about that day, about what my mother did. I have had good fortune in my life. I believe, I just feel it somehow, that the good angel has been with me, always, because of my mother's prayer over my head.*

# Chapter Six

The ten years on and off that he spent in Fargo were formative years for Bennie Berger. Even during the time he was learning to speak English, and then improving his speech, it was clear that he was already developing from a determined but raw, untrained youth into a confident, perceptive young man. Suave and polished he wasn't. He was bold and brash, with sure instincts and a keen appetite for business.

"Overthrow the capitalists!" was a cry he had heard back at the secret meetings in Warsaw. But Berger was enthralled with the free enterprise system. Actually, to be part of it made him even more euphoric than he had dreamed; he beamed in on it like a homing pigeon, feeling as if untied from ropes that previously had been strangling his initiative and hopes.

Not that he would have completely smooth sailing after being released into the mainstream of American life. There would be problems. Unfulfilling jobs. Layoffs. Disagreements with associates. "Sure, I've lost a few hands," he was to say years later, using an analogy befitting one who was known to relish a friendly wager or poker game, "but it's how you're sitting, what you have, at the end of the game that counts." Thus Berger was never overly shaken by an occasional setback, not during the formative decade or in any decade thereafter. He never assumed that the freedom to succeed in America was a guarantee of success. The possibility of failure always existed, although the confident, sometimes even cocky, Ben Berger was sure that in the long run *he* wasn't going to be the person who failed. From the very moment he set out for the United States, he was wrapped in his own personal cocoon of optimism. Even the voyage itself, with its concomitant physical hardships and mental anxieties, was not enough to discourage him.

After saying their goodbyes at the depot in Ostrowiec, Berger, his uncle, and his two cousins had boarded the train that would take them to a point just across the border into Germany. Ben was traveling "light," carrying with him almost literally only the clothes on his back—his "luggage" consisted of one extra shirt.

They spent the night in the depot at their first stop, slept on tables, took another train to Hamburg, where they remained for two days, and then went by boat to their port of embarkation, Liverpool. An eleven-day voyage to Quebec eventually followed under conditions which were apalling, yet typical. With tens of thousands of immigrants clamoring to leave, steamship companies crammed their holds with as much human cargo as possible. Far below deck, third-class passengers, the lowest form of ocean-traveling species, scarcely had room to move, and breathed foul, poorly ventilated air reeking with the mixed stench of sweat and vomit.

Yet these were merely minor inconveniences to Berger. "Everything is relative in this world," he says.

"Compared to what I had left behind, I was very happy to be aboard that ship." He remembers first-and second-class passengers looking down through an opening at the immigrants. They would throw food and other items down to them, as if tossing peanuts through the bars to animals in a zoo. But Berger didn't take offense. He caught a banana—the first he had ever seen—thrown by one passenger. "It tasted pretty good to me," he recalls.

Finally, they were in Quebec. It was a scene of seemingly endless lines, people chattering in a bedlam of a dozen languages and babies wailing in their common language, hard benches, lethargic immigration authorities, an eternity of waiting. For Berger, sitting with the note, "Fargo, North Dakota," pinned to his lapel, there was an extra delay. A medical examination indicated that he might have glaucoma. The authorities refused to let him leave; his uncle and cousins went on without him.

Berger's stomach churned, but not from being left behind and alone. That didn't bother him, and he felt no resentment. Everyone was on his own when getting out of the prison that was Poland, he told himself. The turmoil within him arose instead from the possibility that he would be turned away at the very doorway to his dream. That would have been difficult to take, even for a perennial optimist.

Fortunately, another examination two days later showed that the medical alarm was false. Soon he was on his way to Chicago, where he changed trains for the twenty-four-hour ride to Fargo. On September 1, 1913, he arrived at the Great Northern Railway station, excited and eager to grapple with new adventures. He had one extra shirt and $6.50 in his pocket, 50¢ of which he spent for a horse-and-buggy ride to the home of the Idlekope family,

relatives of the uncle who had married his mother's sister. It was a tenuous connection, but it was all he had. To the Idlekopes, the arrival of this cheerful, toughminded youth brought back memories. They, too, had come out of the same type of *shtetl* ten or more years before, and they appreciated the magnitude of the struggle that lay ahead for the newcomer, because they had gone through it themselves. In fact, they were still struggling. Two of the adult sons in the family, Harry and Joe, were partners in a small confectionery store. There was a bed in the back of the store, where Ben slept for a few nights until he found a room of his own. Meanwhile, Harry, the older brother, had assumed the unofficial role of employment counselor.
 "What can you do, kid?" he asked Berger in Yiddish.
 "I can do anything," replied Berger spunkily. "And if I don't know how to do it, I can learn."
 So he learned. During those initial years in Fargo, he learned how to sell fruit from the side of a railroad car, to pack hay or straw into collars for horse harnesses, to assist the undertaker at Murphy's Catholic mortuary, and to mix candy in huge vats at the Chaney-Everhart Candy Company. He considered the work in the candy factory as his first "profession" because it was his first steady job; he earned seven dollars a week for working 8 A.M. to 6 P.M. weekdays, and 8 to 1 Saturdays. In the evenings, he got another job setting pins in a bowling alley, which brought him an additional four or five dollars a week.
 Eventually he was laid off at the candy factory, and he decided to go to Minneapolis to look for work. He found it as a candy mixer in the Roach-Tisdale factory. After two months, however, the smoke in the plant was bothering him so much that he was sent to a free medical clinic. The doctor said that the smoke was affecting his eyes, and

advised him to quit his job. With reluctance, Berger did. "It was the first job I ever quit. The other times I got fired or laid off."

After a brief period selling newspapers and magazines on the Minneapolis and St. Louis Railroad train between Minneapolis and Chicago, he returned to Fargo, which he now viewed as his "home town." He and Harry Idlekope had another chat. "How about getting a pushcart and peddling fruit that way?" proposed Harry.

Berger (by now the "Beryl" had been officially replaced by "Benjamin" and he was called "Bennie" or "Ben") mulled over the suggestion, tried it for a month, and then he told Idlekope, "I got an idea."

Rather than pushing the cart aimlessly up one street and down another, his idea was to stake out a spot in front of the Orpheum Theater. At that time, snacks were not sold inside theaters. So, Berger thought, why not sell oranges, apples, and other fruit to people as they went in? It seemed like a good idea—until the second night, when he was arrested.

"To this day, I don't know why," he says. "Maybe I was supposed to have had a license, but the police didn't tell me that. Nobody told me anything." He added that he was "plenty boiled" when he got out of jail the next morning. "They gave me back my cart, but all the fruit was gone."

There was no official charge, and Ben knew enough not to press the issue of the "misplaced" fruit. The incident, however, ensured his disenchantment with the pushcart business, which hadn't captured his fancy in the first place. Perhaps it was too much like the past he had escaped from; he was searching for a vocation with a future, not one that reminded him of his father's uncovered wagon.

As he searched, he continued to find new jobs. He was like a man panning for gold, not knowing how or where he would discover it, but certain of making a strike eventually if he tried long enough and hard enough. In the process, he was gaining invaluable experience and developing contacts that would be helpful later.

Also, the inherent traits that would characterize the mature Ben Berger were beginning to show. You just couldn't keep the ebullient fellow down—he kept resurfacing like a cork—and you couldn't stay mad at him. In a business career that has occupied most of this century, Berger has had many flamboyant outbursts and spectacular confrontations. Yet he has relatively few, if any, personal enemies. He carries no grudges himself, and if he has antagonized his foes on occasion, they still can't help but admire his tenacity, honesty, and sincerity.

One of Berger's initial confrontations came soon after the pushcart debacle. Harry Idlekope had bought another confectionery store on Front Street, in Fargo. Ben was brought in to run the place as a partner. He slept in a room upstairs of the store and drew only enough salary to meet his living expenses. When Idlekope sold the store eight months later, Ben did not get the money he thought was due him as a partner. The two had some words before Idlekope finally gave him fifty dollars. Meanwhile, Ben had had to find another place to live, and in this respect he was fortunate. He moved in with the Burt and Rebecca Hartstein family, where he was made to feel wanted and welcome rather than like just another roomer. "It was my first home away from home," he says.

Despite Berger's disagreement with Harry Idlekope, there were no lasting hard feelings; in fact, he continued to work for a time in Idlekope's other store. Next he delivered food by horse and wagon for wholesale distributors. He was employed first by the Gillis and Naftalin Wholesale Fruit Company. When the two owners split up, he worked

for Gillis, then for Naftalin, and then for Gillis again. During one period with Gillis, he lived in a caboose while escorting a railroad-car load of potatoes from Thief River Falls, Minnesota, to Chicago.
If the ex-partners ever took umbrage at Berger's flexible loyalty, they didn't voice it. Employees as smart and reliable as Bennie were hard to find. They would have been spiting themselves by rejecting his services merely because he was willing to work for whichever one wanted him most.

\* \* \*

Thanks to the consistent demand for his services, Ben had saved $101 by 1917. It wasn't a princely sum but, as Berger would say, "everything is relative." It was enough to enable him to consider starting an independent business. After he saw an empty store on Broadway, about a block from the store he used to sleep in, he began to make his plans.

The budding young entrepreneur had to do some figuring to be certain that he could finance his new venture. Rent was twenty-five dollars a month. The store needed painting; that would cost twelve dollars. He could get fruits on credit from Gillis for a week, and have them sold within that time. He had to have candy, cigars, and cigarettes. Buying that inventory required half payment in advance, the other half in a week. He wanted to put a mirror in back of the soda fountain. The price was $150, but he could make an agreement to pay $10 down and $10 a month.

There wasn't much left of his savings by the time the door opened to "Bennie Berger's," the newest confectionery store in Fargo. Ben, however, had a solution. While delivering for the wholesale fruit company, he had become friendly with some restaurant owners. He went to two or three of these contacts and sold them on the idea of buying fruit from him at cost. Although there was no profit in the transaction itself, he got the fruit on credit, received cash from the restaurants, and used that cash as operating capital. Ah, capitalism! It was wonderful. Berger loved it. About a year later, the call came for him to be drafted into the army. He wasn't really eligible for the draft at that point, because he hadn't been in the country for the five years required for citizenship. Nevertheless, he didn't hesitate. He sold the store for $1,500, which gave him a total savings of $1,550. He then sent $500 to his parents, put $1,000 into a savings account, and took the rest with him into military service. Not long after, he became a citizen, getting his papers while at Camp Custer in Battle Creek, Michigan.

It was a measure of Berger's patriotism that he had agreed to be drafted before he was a citizen. Given the option of entering the army or staying in business, it was obvious to him what his choice would be, or, to more accurately describe his frame of mind, there *was* no choice. He was committed to America, and he was accepting his responsibility, just as he was committed to helping his parents financially as soon as he was able.

"I was, and am, very idealistic," he says. "I went into service because I believed in the philosophy of America. Those people at the meetings in Warsaw put that belief in me, even though that's not what they were trying to do. I wasn't ready to fight the Czar, but I was ready to fight for the United States of America."

There was a fleeting period initially when Berger's fighting spirit uncharacteristically evaporated. He was one of fifty recruits boarding the troop train, which had stopped in Fargo, enroute from the West Coast to Camp Custer, a basic training camp. All of the other recruits had had family and friends at the railroad station to see them off. Ben was the only one with nobody to kiss him goodbye and to wish him well. For some reason, this affected him much more than the heart-wrenching experience of leaving his family in Ostrowiec.

"I began—truly for the first time—to feel blue, lonesome, and sorry for myself," he admits. "I didn't want to talk to any of the other fellows, and when I went to bed, I actually started crying. I covered my face so the others wouldn't notice and think I was a sissy, and I actually cried myself to sleep."

But Berger was by nature an optimist and positive thinker. By the next morning, his bout with self-pity was over. Later there would be another brief spell of loneliness brought on by watching others get mail. Ben received only one letter—from the Hartstein family—through his entire year of army service. After experiencing disappointment a few times, however, he shrugged it off and simply didn't attend mail calls anymore. Aside from that, his service tenure for the most part was a positive experience, affording him previously unavailable opportunities to sample fresh slices of American life.

There was, for example, a twenty-four-hour pass to New York City, which he received while on the way to Camp Upton in New York, prior to being shipped overseas. Berger and a fellow soldier walked, open-mouthed and wide-eyed, amidst the big buildings and theaters and other attractions of Forty-second Street, Fifth Avenue, and Broadway. They had hot dogs and cokes for dinner—it tasted delicious—and then they stopped for two or three dances at a ten-cent-a-dance emporium. They took pictures in a picture gallery until about 3 A.M., after which, with no money left to rent a hotel room, they ended up sleeping on benches in Grand Central Station. Salvation Army personnel woke them up at 8 A.M., fed them doughnuts and coffee, and two hours later they resumed their trip to Camp Upton, tired but euphoric.

But Berger's most vivid memories of army life concern a series of episodes that told him that his mother's blessing, made with upstretched arms over his head just before he had left Poland, was still working. The good angel, he was convinced, was still watching over him.

He recalls being stricken suddenly with an epidemiclike flu and high temperature. Lying in a military hospital bed at Camp Upton, he looked out the window and saw a large quantity of big, rectangular boxes. A nurse indelicately informed Ben that the boxes were for carrying off hospital patients, who were dying all around him from the same strange flu. This was hardly comforting information, but Ben's fever and flu inexplicably disappeared after forty-eight hours and he was released, alive and hearty, from the hospital.

A few weeks later, he was on his way to France with fifty thousand replacement troops in a twenty-ship convoy—eighteen troop ships with one destroyer leading and another in back. The journey to Liverpool, England took twelve days because of the convoy's zig-zagging course to avoid submarines. Then there was several days' delay in England while transportation was being arranged to get them across the Channel; that was ultimately accomplished, says Berger, on boats so crowded that "when we slept, somebody was using my leg as a pillow and my head was on someone else's leg."

The day Berger's contingent arrived in France, there was great excitement as the U.S. doughboys marched through the town of Le Havre. Whistles shrieked. Automobile horns blew. Church bells rang. Bottles of wine were passed through the marching ranks; a soldier would take a drink and pass the bottle to his buddy next to him.

"We didn't know what all the commotion was about," says Berger. "I thought that the French were just happy to

## Thank You, America 57

see Americans. But when we reached camp, we found out that the armistice had just been signed."

It was good fortune indeed to have been delayed long enough in transit so that the war ended on the day he got there, November 11, 1918. The angel was still being good to him, Berger nodded to himself.

He would have felt even better about his circumstances that day, had he been able to get something to eat. The doughboys had eaten an early dinner before marching to camp, and they had missed breakfast the next morning. So they had hearty appetites when they sat down for lunch. Heaping platters of food were dispatched along the various rows of hungry soldiers. But Berger, as luck would have it, was at the end of a row. Each time a platter got to him, it was empty. Soon lunch was over and he still hadn't eaten. He complained to the mess sergeant, who was somewhat less than sympathetic. "This is a rest camp," he barked to Berger. "You're supposed to rest your stomach." Which Ben did, albeit grudgingly, until he had better luck at dinner time.

Not long afterward, however, he was more than consoled by his assignment to the censor's office in Paris. The job of censoring letters written by American soldiers was, to him, a plum. It gave him the opportunity to improve his English, which was still not the best, and when the day's work was done he was free to come and go as he liked.

One evening, while having dinner at a Jewish restaurant, Ben found himself sitting next to an American soldier from Brooklyn. On the other side of the American was a Polish Jewish soldier, who was trying to sell a fancy revolver taken off a German officer. Berger wasn't paying much attention, until suddenly he heard a bang, and a scream. The revolver had been loaded, and in testing it the Polish soldier had shot the American in the heart.

Ben raced outside, found a taxi, helped carry the wounded man into it, and took him to the hospital. Seated in the back with the man, he tried to comfort him. But he only heard him say one word.

"Mommy!" the American cried.

"I visited him the next night," recalls Berger. "He couldn't talk. The night after that, I went again. He wasn't there—he had died that day." Berger paused in the telling. "That was a tragic moment."

The tragedy sharpened Ben's awareness of his own luck, being stationed in Paris and encountering what he felt was one favorable omen after another. He remembers, for example, attending a memorial observance in Paris with other American soldiers. President Woodrow Wilson was the speaker. In what seemed to be another lifetime— although it was actually only a few short years before, in 1912—Ben had read about Wilson's election. He had been so impressed then by the freedom in the United States, and now, here he was, an American citizen, sitting two rows behind President Wilson himself.

"It was almost unbelievable to me that I was close enough to the president of the United States to be able to reach out and touch him," Berger says. "The president spoke about the importance of our soldiers not having given their lives in vain. I was very much taken by this subject, and his speech was the most touching I had ever heard."

\* \* \*

A different Ben Berger returned home to Fargo than the person who had first arrived, right off the boat, fresh and green as a just-picked cucumber. He had never lacked confidence, but before there had been a touch of bravado in his demeanor. After all, he hadn't really accomplished anything by that time, so his self-assurance had been rooted in theory, not fact. Now, he was a man instead of a youth. He could speak English. He was a citizen and a veteran of the United States Army. And there was another difference. He had arrived from Poland in debt, if one wanted to be technical about it, because he owed his father for the boat fare, and with $6.50 in his pocket. Now, in July 1919, he was returning to a bank balance of $1,000; he had already sent Chaim Berger $500, which more than cleared up the debt (although he would never stop sending money home), and he had $500 in his pocket—thanks in part to a hot streak during a game of craps on the voyage home. Ben was ready to roll up his sleeves and take a very large bite into his share of the free enterprise system. "Nothing can stop me now," he said to himself.

Such cockiness could leave one ill-prepared to cope with the inevitable rude shocks and surprises awaiting any businessman. But although Berger was occasionally knocked off his pedestal, he took it with good grace and simply climbed back up again. Moreover, his optimism about his future in Fargo was soon justified. Moving boldly and swiftly, before long he had three confectionery stores and was viewed as one of the rising young small-businessmen of the city.

His "damn the torpedoes" attitude led him to take whatever action was required in order to keep moving ahead. One of his stores was a former ladies' and children's wear shop. He had to buy the inventory in order to get the location, paying $2,500, even though his knowledge of ladies' and children's wear was minimal. But he held a sale to clear out the inventory and before the doors to the confectionery store had even opened he had his money back, and then some. Another time, he bought a pool hall a few doors away from one of his stores, so that he would have a convenient place to store furniture, candy cases, and soda fountains.

The flagship of his minichain was the "Bennie Berger's" on Broadway, near the Great Northern Railway Station. Knowing that trains arrived at various hours of the day and night, Berger conceived the idea—revolutionary for its time in Fargo—of staying open twenty-four hours a day. He hired women—girls, actually—to work three to a shift, 8 A.M. to 4 P.M., 4 P.M. to midnight, and midnight to 8 A.M., and paid them up to twenty-five dollars a week, a liberal wage then. With typical Berger aplomb, he shrugged off the progressing metamorphosis of Polish immigrant into capitalist. "I always felt that it was just a matter of time," he once said, "before I would be employing people."

Berger, of course, worked himself harder than he did any of his employees. He was at the store from 9 A.M. to midnight, after which he gathered the receipts (usually from seventy-five to ninety dollars, mostly in change) in a sack and peddled home on his bicycle. He was living then, as he had for two years before serving in the army, with Burt and Rebecca Hartstein, people whom he remembers with fondness. "Becky Hartstein was like a second mother to me," he recalls. "I considered her my American mother."

One night he gave his "American mother" substantial cause for concern when he was unusually late getting home. He had fallen asleep on his bicycle, run into a curb, and flown head over heels to the ground. After lying stunned for awhile, Ben had finally collected himself and his change, and peddled home, aching from embarrassment as well as physical damage. Falling asleep on a bicycle was not the most impressive act for a blossoming business tycoon.

\* \* \*

At this stage of his career, although possessing abundant vision and a pioneering free enterprise instinct, Ben was nonetheless uncertain about future projects. Clearly he was not going to be running confectionery stores all his life. He knew that he was destined for bigger and better challenges, depending on how quickly his accumulation of capital matched his ambition. But he had nothing specific in mind—it remained for old-fashioned coincidence to show him the way.

Across the street from the store where Berger spent most of his time was the Strand, a movie theater. It was owned by two Jewish men who were frequently in Berger's place to buy candy or tobacco or just to "schmoose." He admired them and thought they were "real live wires."

One of the theater owners, John Goldsman, was equally impressed with Ben. One live wire evidently recognized another. Goldsman approached him with a proposition. "Bennie, I hear that the Strand Theater in Grand Forks is for sale. How would you like to go into partnership with me and buy it?"

"A motion picture theater?" Berger hesitated. "I've never been in that business before. I don't know anything about it, and I don't know anything about motion pictures."

"I do," Goldsman said. "And besides, I've seen you in action. You're a natural promoter. You could learn the business."

Berger nodded. That was the boast he had made to Harry Idlekope nine years before, when he had first arrived and Harry was looking for a job for him. He could learn, all right. Hadn't he proved it? Of course, a confectionery store was no theater. Selling candy and ice cream and cigarettes, items customers could taste and smell, was far different from trying to entertain people. Movies were *show business*.

On the other hand, he suddenly realized that the very thought of being in show business had started him tingling, for some strange reason. He felt as if he were about to climb the highest mountain. But, he knew one had to be practical, too.

"How much do they want?" he asked, coming back down to earth.

"Nine thousand," answered Goldsman. "Believe me, it's a good price."

"Maybe," said Berger. "Okay, let's go see it."

They drove to Grand Forks, about ninety miles north of Fargo, and checked out the property. Once he was there, looking at the theater, his mind probing and analyzing, Berger found that his doubts had vanished. Showing pictures was a cash business, just like his confectionery stores. The principle was the same: you buy right, you sell right, you give the people what they want, you treat them right. There was nothing difficult or esoteric about operating a motion picture theater, he decided.

Of course, this was before he became a sophisticate in the exhibiting business. This was before he found out about the arm-twisting, the squeeze plays, the financial pressure that could be exerted on exhibitors by giant movie studios. Bennie Berger, having determined that he should proceed to buy the Strand Theater with John Goldsman, was in for a lesson in a phase of the free enterprise system hitherto unknown to him.

But then, so were the movie studios. They would not have believed it possible to have so much difficulty with a tiny, independent exhibitor from, of all places, North Dakota. There would be times when they wished that they had never heard of Benjamin N. Berger.

## Chapter Seven

The motion picture industry in its early stages did not boast a prestigious reputation. As an art form, it was given short shrift by devotees of the legitimate stage. Moreover, from the standpoint of the elite and the cultured, movies were somewhat suspect because of the "distasteful" element to which they appealed. They were popular with immigrants and other "common folk," who found them a convenient and inexpensive form of escapist entertainment. Not only that, but the industry in the 1920s was even ruled, for the most part, either by immigrants or by rough-edged individuals who had come from poor immigrant families.

Many of these movie moguls were Jewish, such as Louis B. Mayer, Marcus Loewe, Adolph Zukor, and William Fox. That was proof enough for some people that "Hebrew genes were at work," and that they had cause to fear "international conspiracy" or other vague and threatening consequences. What the Jewish movie mogul really represented, of course, was the coincidental juxtaposition of the emerging film technology and the flood of immigration in the decades just before and just after the turn of the century.

The new industry attracted a pioneering breed. In order to survive, a filmmaker needed the nerve of a gambler and the fighting instincts of a combat soldier. Such an arena was hardly the place for the refined, the scholarly, or the fainthearted. Lack of education, lack of status, and occasional broken English were not insurmountable barriers in this industry, and the movie business was well suited to those who didn't mind taking a risk because they had nothing to lose. In short, it was a provocative beacon for newcomers to this land of opportunity, and for determined have-nots of any origin, Jewish or otherwise.

Indeed, one of the movie impresarios whom Bennie Berger was to admire the most was not a Jew from Eastern Europe but a Greek, Spyros Skouras, president of 20th Century-Fox. It wasn't only that they were contemporaries— Skouras was just four years older than Berger—or that both had emigrated to the United States as penniless teenagers. What Berger admired about Skouras was his scrappy willingness to face hostile groups.

When Skouras agreed to speak at the Allied States Association convention of theater owners in 1955, it was like Gary Cooper single-handedly facing the enemy in *High Noon*. Berger was also a featured speaker, because he was president of North Central Allied, a constituent exhibitor organization. The appearance of the two men on the same dais was the subject of an article in *Variety*, the entertainment trade newspaper, under the headline, "Skouras, Daniel in Lion's Den, A Match for Allied's Berger In Lincoln-Douglas 'Dialectics.' "

"Emerging as the dominant figures of last week's Allied States Association convention in Chicago," the article began, "were two men in opposite camps—Spyros Skouras, the expressive prez of 20th-Fox, and Bennie Berger, the highly articulate and opinionated head of North

Central Allied." *Variety* pointed out that "interestingly, both men seem to show tremendous admiration for each other's ability," adding that each was "a practiced orator, capable of arousing and swaying an audience. Later in the article, there was a description of Skouras's courage at addressing an audience "out for his scalp," and Berger was quoted as saying, "He's the only company president who has the guts to appear before this convention. You don't see any other bloodsuckers here."

It was not lost on Skouras that the remark indirectly tarred him with the same brush as his fellow presidents—the only difference being that he was characterized as a brave bloodsucker instead of just a plain bloodsucker. Yet he did not take offense because he realized that Berger, in his own way, really was paying him tribute. He knew that Berger respected him, and he felt the same way about the combative theater owner.

Actually, a strange form of understanding and wary camaraderie existed between Ben and most film producers and distributors. Although his colorful descriptions and often torrid charges hardly endeared him to them (a fact which did not cause Berger to lose any sleep at night), few of them resented him to the point of a permanent feud. A Minneapolis exhibitor, Martin Lebedoff, once explained it this way:

"The studios respected anyone who would stand up to them. If theater owners would allow it, the studios would run all over them. But if you were strong enough and willing enough to fight, that was something they could understand."

\* \* \*

Conflict was a way of life in the movie industry, although this hadn't always been the case. Early in the century, film production companies were one big happy family when they started shooting in southern California, where they went not only because of the weather but because of the diversity of natural outdoor scenery within the immediate area. All of the participants in the new venture—actors, directors, cameramen—shared a bond of happy ignorance. No one really knew what he was doing and, what's more, everybody knew that everybody else was in the same predicament. So they struggled along cheerily together and, for many of them, the entire experience was a lark.

Some didn't even believe that the motion picture industry was permanent, so their main concern was to have a good time while the venture lasted. The only people who weren't happy were the residents of California. They were horrified to find movie actors in their midst, and they didn't even want to rent houses or apartments to them. This, too, served to build a spirit of togetherness among the participants.

It wasn't until artistic and creative temperaments began to take hold, until the star system began to evolve, until the realization dawned that a tremendous sum of money could be made from movies that the spirit of togetherness unraveled like a ball of yarn. The battles started—actors against directors, exhibitors against distributors, studios against studios, not to mention struggles for control within studios and even one attempt by a combine, which included Thomas Alva Edison, to control the entire industry.

Edison held the first patent on motion pictures, but originally he considered the invention to be little more than a toy. Gradually new patents were granted to others, and film moved from the "kinetoscope parlors" (penny arcades containing individual viewing machines) of the 1890s, to makeshift theaters. Edison realized that others were profiting more from his invention, or variations thereof, than he was. In January 1909, his company joined with seven other leading filmmakers—Biograph, Essanay, Kalem, Kleine, Lubin, Selig and Vitagraph—plus two French companies, Pathe and Melies, to form the Motion Picture Patents Company (MPPC). Through this trust and the distributing organization it subsequently set up, an attempt was made to monopolize the manufacture of film, use of projection equipment, and rights to obtain motion pictures. The objective was to force exhibitors to deal only with MPPC under rental terms established by MPPC.

The independents resisted the effort furiously. Two of the leaders in this opposition were Carl Laemmle and William Fox, who operated theaters called nickelodeons in Chicago, and New York, respectively. The weapons of their counter-movement included lawsuits, advertisements aimed at arousing the ire of the public, and discovery of new film sources outside of MPPC. Laemmle and Fox, among others, also sharpened another tool to use against the monopoly—they started making films themselves. Laemmle was the founder of Universal Company, which subsequently became Universal International. Fox's production company in later years was merged into 20th Century Pictures, the studio founded by Joseph Schenck and Darryl F. Zanuck, to become 20th Century-Fox.

The combination of vigorous dissent by leaders such as Laemmle and Fox and the shaky legal position of the Motion Picture Patents Company led to the official demise of the trust in 1915. By then, other battles were springing up within the industry like brush fires. Some individuals were becoming bigger than the studios. Four of them, Douglas Fairbanks, Mary Pickford, Charlie Chaplin, and D. W. Griffith, a director whose credits included *Birth Of A Nation*, broke away in 1919 to launch their own studio, United Artists.

The idea of artistic types actually trying to run a business struck some film people as absurd. "The lunatics have taken charge of the asylum," cracked Richard Rowland, head of production at Marcus Loewe's Metro Pictures.

But although some developments might have been fodder for jokes, there was also a more serious, smoldering, dangerous side to the industry. It was not uncommon for aggressive, short-tempered studio executives to resort to physical violence when angered. Louis Mayer once punched Charlie Chaplin, knocking him down, after an exchange of words in a Los Angeles hotel. Nor were goon squads unknown. Some independents had had their equipment wrecked when they attempted to revolt against the Motion Picture Patents Company, and such violence did not stop with the death of MPPC.

Studios that owned movie theaters were not adverse to making threats against independent theater owners. Exhibitors were not above retaliation. Ben Berger knows of one who advised a motion picture company not to build a theater next to the exhibitor's "or you'll have a fire before you open." It was language the film company understood; the theater was never built.

\* \* \*

Berger's own confrontations began not long after he and John Goldsman bought the Strand Theater in Grand Forks. The Strand had not proved as promising as at first blush. Its books were incomplete, and at closer inspection, the profit picture suddenly looked bleak. There was also tough competition from three other theaters in town. Goldsman began to get "cold feet," in Berger's words. "I don't know, Bennie," the older man mused doubtfully. "Maybe this wasn't such a hot deal after all."

Those were fighting words to Berger, who wasn't as readily inclined to concede that he had entered into a bad

investment. "It just takes time," he consoled Goldsman.
"But we're losing money here."
"I can turn this place around," said Ben confidently. Goldsman, however, wasn't so sure, and felt that he, after all, was the experienced theater man of the two. He grew increasingly dubious, and Berger, in turn, began to boil with frustration at having to work in such a negative atmosphere. After six months, Berger suggested that he buy his partner out. Goldsman jumped at the offer like a sprinter off the starting block. So Ben borrowed $5,000 from Fargo banker Alex Stern and, in the fall of 1921, became the sole owner of the Strand Theater.

He also temporarily became the manager, having decided that the best and fastest way to turn the Strand around was for him to run it himself. With his confectionery stores in Fargo going smoothly, he moved to Grand Forks, checked into the YMCA, and started poring over trade magazines and other reading material to learn as much as he could about the motion picture industry and about films that people liked to see.

Concurrent with this effort, Ben peered into every nook and cranny of the Strand operation to determine how he could cut costs until the theater was back on its feet. The extent to which he was concerned about costs was illustrated by his first decision, which was to change the telephone from a private line to a party line. This saved him one dollar a month, no small accomplishment during a period when literally every dollar was vital.

The most critical step in the turnabout came when Ben marched forward to confront Paramount, bearing with him the determination to spear the studio with the same royal shaft he felt it was giving his little theater. Even though Berger was a novice in the exhibiting business, he could add and subtract and count the house. It didn't take him long to figure out that, at the prices he was paying Paramount for its films, he couldn't make any money showing them. But when he pointed this out, the reply was, "You have a contract."

"I didn't sign that contract," Ben protested.

"You assumed the obligation when you bought the Strand."

"Well," Berger answered sharply, "I'm not paying those prices and you know what you can do with that contract."

The haggling that ensued was typical for film negotiations of that day. The fact was that motion picture companies realized full well that they were forcing unreasonable demands on many exhibitors. But everyone was fair game. If an exhibitor was unknowing enough or uncertain enough to bow to pressure and sign a clearly inequitable contract, one that practically ensured his drowning in red ink, then that was his problem and he had to suffer the consequences.

If a studio ran into a buzz saw such as Berger, however, it could be prevailed upon to renegotiate a more sensible business arrangement, even when a contract was already in effect. Paramount, after several weeks of verbal warfare, agreed to reduce the rental terms for Berger by $25 a picture. With this new agreement, plus his ability to choose pictures that drew as large or larger audiences than his competition—Ben was making $150 a week profit within a few months.

He was frankly thrilled by his success and by the discovery of a creative outlet attuned to his natural independence and flamboyance. This was the type of career he had been searching for since leaving Poland. The motion picture business was infinitely more satisfying than selling candy, he realized. Later, he would even decry the need for small-town theater owners to have to sell candy and popcorn in their theaters in order to survive economically.

"That's no business for exhibitors," he would say, in castigating the studios for establishing terms that forced exhibitors to supplement income from ticket sales. "We're showmen. That's the business we know. That's where we belong," he would insist.

Of course, Ben was not so inflexible as to allow this opinion to interfere with the realities of life. If all the other exhibitors were going to sell confectionery items, then so would he. There were times when this role demanded ingenious solutions, such as when Berger discovered that people were inserting slugs instead of nickels in his candy vending machine.

He put up a sign stating, "Anyone putting a slug in this machine will have seven years of bad luck." The use of slugs, he recalls, "dropped by seventy-five percent!"

\* \* \*

It was no exaggeration to put motion picture exhibiting into the category of show business. Films had become an extremely popular entertainment medium for the masses. Theater owners bought from people who actually *made movies.* Why, some owners had even *met* the stars of these movies! In the eyes of the general public, especially in small-town America, such magnetism by association greatly enhanced the exhibitors' status. Certainly this was true in the 1920s in Grand Forks, North Dakota, population 14,000.

Small as it was, however, Grand Forks was no cultural desert. It was the home of the University of North Dakota, founded in 1883, only nine years after the town itself was started at the fork where the Red Lake River flowed into the Red River of the North. It had had a daily newspaper since 1881. It was a popular center for debates; one subject before the turn of the century was "whether a young man can marry and live comfortably in Grand Forks on $12 a week" (the negative side won, according to newspaper reports).

But most of all, the citizens of Grand Forks were proud of their Metropolitan Opera House, an elegant brownstone building built in 1890 at a cost of $150,000. With its ivory, blue, and gold baroque decor, impressive auditorium, two curving balconies, luxurious draperies and seats, and large stage, the Metropolitan was a near replica of the then-famous Chicago auditorium. The Metropolitan manager, George Broadhurst, promoted Grand Forks as the lone frontier town stop between Chicago and San Francisco, and he was able to book well-known attractions of the day—Theodore Thomas, John Phillip Sousa, De Wolfe Hopper, Richard Mansfield.

When movies arrived in Grand Forks in 1907, the Metropolitan became a motion picture theater, and the interior was no longer so lavishly maintained. After all, men, women, and children of all classes were now able to enter an opera house that was once the exclusive domain of the socially prominent. Still, the building was the classiest movie theater in town. Most other early theaters in Grand Forks—including Bennie Berger's Strand—were converted stores, as they usually were in other communities. The inside of a store was gutted, wooden seats were installed, a canopy was erected outside, and—presto!—a theater was born.

As movies became bigger and better, the industry began to look askance at the shabby quarters in which films were often being shown. This was no way to woo the public; converted stores, or even converted opera houses for that matter, were not the proper settings for the fantasy world of film. Dissatisfaction gradually led to the design and construction of theaters for the express purpose of exhibiting motion pictures.

One of the innovators was Marcus Loewe, whom Berger was later to know casually. Loewe's Metro Pictures eventually joined forces with Samuel Goldwyn and Louis B. Mayer to form Metro-Goldwyn-Mayer (MGM). But before that, Loewe got his start, as did so many others in the industry, running nickelodeons—in his case, in New York. Like Carl Laemmle and William Fox, he then began making pictures himself, short one- or two-reelers, and showing them in his own small theaters, which generally were former stores. Business was so good that he went to the bank to apply for a loan to build a first-class theater.

As Berger relates the story, the bank was leery and dispatched a representative to California "to see what was going on in this young industry." The representative was appalled. He reported back that "people are making two hundred fifty or three hundred dollars a week out here and running around like chickens with their heads cut off. It's not being operated like a business."

"Loewe agreed with the analysis," says Berger. "He told the bank, 'it *is* a strange business. But it will straighten itself out. And, it's a cash business. Every Monday my theaters tell me how much money we took in, and it's all cash. We don't have to worry about bad debts.' He got his loan, and that was the start of a chain, which included Loewe's State Theater in New York City."

\* \* \*

While Loewe and his counterparts were embarked on their grand designs nationally, a minor dynasty of sorts was emerging out of the Red River Valley area of North Dakota. By late 1923, Ben Berger had sold his confectionery stores and moved to Grand Forks permanently with his new wife, the former Beatrice Gillis, daughter of his ex-employer in the wholesale fruit business in Fargo.

Ben threw himself into his new career with unabashed enthusiasm, combined with a sound sense of showmanship. He started Berger Amusement Company, and within five years the company had two more theaters in Grand Forks, the Metropolitan and the Orpheum, and had expanded into other communities, operating two theaters in Bemidji, Minnesota and one each in Hallock, Minnesota and Sioux Falls, South Dakota.

He was now among the "Who's Who" of Grand Forks—a highly successful businessman in his early thirties, vice commander of the American Legion, active in the Lions and the Forty and Eight, president of Red River Valley Lodge Number 966 of B'nai B'rith. It was during this period that, for the first time, he experienced recognition as a public figure, as a celebrity in his own right. Then as now, he never made any secret of his affinity for publicity. It thrilled him. What he did made news, and making news was what he did; he was his own best press agent.

He became a promoter of live acts as well as a theater exhibitor, using his Metropolitan Opera House to present attractions such as Will Rogers, Houdini, Fritz Kreisler, Schuman Heink, the Minneapolis Symphony Orchestra, and various theatrical road shows. No facet of the entertainment world was beyond his scope. If the public wanted it, if it would sell tickets, he would provide it—which is how and why he became a boxing and wrestling promoter as well. He even managed boxers; one of his fighters, welterweight Johnny Knauff, fought two matches—granted, they were losing ones—with the highly rated "Fargo Express," Billy Petrolle. In the small pond that was Grand Forks, Ben Berger was beyond question a big fish. He was the undisputed impresario of the area.

It was once suggested to Berger that, with his flair for entertaining the public, he could well have been a big fish in a big pond, particularly if circumstances had treated him differently. Instead of winding up in North Dakota, what if he had emigrated from Poland to the East Coast, the heart of the nickelodeon district that spawned tycoons such as Marcus Loewe, or to California, where the film industry grew up? Would he then have wound up in the arms of the movie studios rather than at arm's length from them? Perhaps he would even have owned a studio himself.

Although he relishes the thought of such a stimulating challenge, Berger probably would have been ill suited to the Hollywood environment. He could not even have pretended to be cast in the mold of the typical studio tyrant or mogul, personified by executives such as Harry Cohn, founder of Columbia Studios. It was a measure of Cohn's relationships that, when he died in 1958, comedian Red Skelton, in an oft-repeated line, remarked about the large attendance at the funeral, "It only proves what they always say—give the public what they want to see and they'll come out for it."

Berger has never been regarded with such contempt. His personal battles notwithstanding, he was always sensitive about the rights and aspirations of others, especially those less able or less fortunate than he. Not that he was a saint or entirely altruistic when engaged, for example, in bitter competition against other exhibitors—such as the Baehr Brothers in Bemidji or Finkelstein and Ruben in Grand Forks. And certainly his self-interests were served when he motivated his supporters to battle studios that were supplying his competitors with films that he wanted.

Still, he could argue with justification that, even in those instances, he was speaking for small, independent exhibitors who wanted only the opportunity to earn a reasonable living, without fear of being crushed by the heavy-handed giants.

Martin Lebedoff, who deeply admires Berger as "an unusually fine human being," points out that "some of the people who ran theaters in little towns were like children against the film industry. Bennie fought for those people. He helped them, protected them, organized buyers' strikes, saw to it that they bought pictures at the right prices."

Thus Berger almost invariably was embroiled in controversy. Whenever a proposal was made that, in his view, threatened the "little guy," he rode forward to the defense and dispatched pithy messages to the offending studio, such as when he wrote a film company, "The next time you come up with an idea like this, please do it on softer paper." Once Joseph Schenck, then of United Artists, proposed as an economy measure that film company salesmen no longer be sent to towns with a population under 4,000. Ben reacted as if stung by a bee.

"If the smallest exhibitors from North Dakota and South Dakota have to go to Minneapolis to make their film deals, this will put an additional expense burden on those who can least afford any increase in operating costs," he charged in successfully squelching the proposal. "We all know that any savings by distributors from such a plan will never be passed on to the exhibitors."

In 1935, he even took on the independent theater owners organization of which he was a member, when it adopted a resolution that film service be discontinued to theaters charging less than fifteen cents admission. The purpose was to eliminate the "dime houses." But Berger argued—again successfully—that independents had always fought for the principle that theater owners should be able to purchase product with no restrictions from distributors on admission prices.

"What about the Minneapolis ten-cent Gateway theaters, which are patronized entirely by the poorest classes?"

he asked. "Besides, this is a competitive, creative business. Why box it up into a set of rules and play into the hands of producer-owned chains who have the advantage in obtaining product. Take the creativeness away from the independent and you'll kick hell out of our business."

\* \* \*

There was no question that motion picture exhibiting was a business that Ben Berger cared about most deeply. He firmly believed that there should be a theater in every town. He was committed to the viability of film as an entertainment medium and to the ability of exhibitors—at least those who were true showmen—to sell tickets to the public. "There's never a depression for good pictures," was one of his claims.

His faith and confidence in the product of film were not always shared by the people who were responsible for producing films. He was once at a meeting in Hollywood with Dore Schary, executive in charge of production for MGM. Berger and Schary had had philosophical differences before; the latter was a believer in "message" pictures.

"Please, Mr. Schary," Ben told him. "Let Western Union deliver the messages and let us entertain the public."

Yet even Berger would have admitted that if anyone had the qualifications to accurately analyze the industry, it was Dore Schary. He had started as a $100-a-week scriptwriter with Columbia Pictures in 1932, went on to win an Oscar for the screenplay of *Boys Town* in 1938, became a producer for David O. Selznick, was a vice-president at RKO Pictures—his credits went on and on. So Ben was surprised, at the meeting, when a man of such stature expressed doubt about the future of motion pictures.

It was during the early days of television. "This just might kill the business," lamented Schary.

"I don't see why," Berger protested. "I think television can even be a good thing for us. We can buy advertising on it to sell our movies."

"Ben, people who have a television set will have a theater right in their home. Why should they go out to a movie?"

"Well, every home has a kitchen," Ben shot back, "but that doesn't mean that the restaurant business isn't any good."

It wasn't television that Berger feared, any more than his faith in movies had been shaken during the depression years earlier. What did bother him was the composition of the industry itself. The establishment. The power structure.

Ben had adopted some of the appurtenances of the industry, of the showman, of the mogul. He had the big desk. He had started smoking the finest cigars (and to this day is still seldom seen without one). He enjoyed having prestige and influence just as much as did Harry Cohn and others of that ilk. Where Ben differed, however, was in his fundamental belief that power shouldn't be unfairly used to stamp out the less powerful.

He had rebelled against the life he knew in Poland, and he was still a rebel. Very early on, there was a voice in his psyche that drove him to confront the entrenched—he always seemed to be part of the opposition. A "cause" man with an innate sympathy for the underdog, his first cause had been himself, and America had given him the freedom to develop his potential. But that was only the beginning, and the same spirit and compassion that led him to fight for weaker exhibitors, who couldn't help themselves, probably would have precluded his ever becoming part of the Hollywood Establishment.

He fulfilled what he felt were his responsibilities, even if it meant going to lengths that the average movie mogul would have considered masochistic. In order to attend a regional meeting of North Central Allied, the independent theater owners group of which he was president, Berger once took a fifty-mile journey out of Bismarck, North Dakota on a freight train with passenger car attached. He was traveling with Stanley Kane, then general counsel for the group, and later a district court judge. The train left Bismarck at 7 A.M., and over the course of a five-hour ride, stopped at every hamlet along the way to drop off milk or pick up empty cans.

Along about 11 A.M., the seat-sore passengers stared wearily at each other. "You know, Stan," sighed Berger, "just before I left Europe, my mother told me there would be days like this." Then he smiled. "But thank God, she said there would be better ones, too."

Benjamin Berger's parents, Roza and Chaim Berger, died in the Holocaust along with Ben's two sisters and their husbands and children.

Corporal Benjamin Berger posed in front of the Rheims Cathedral in Paris in 1918.

This photo from 1938 was among the last pictures taken of Roza Berger.

Bennie Berger was pictured in July, 1920 with one of his early employees, Elizabeth Zimerman.

A happy group of Minneapolis Lakers (Ben Berger is at the left, foreground) celebrated after winning the professional basketball championship in 1952. It was one of six titles captured by the Lakers under the ownership of Berger and his partners.

Six foot, 10 inch George Mikan, shown with Ben and Midge Berger, was known as "Mr. Basketball" during his championship playing days with the Minneapolis Lakers from the late 1940s until the middle 1950s.

This was the 1960-61 contingent of Minneapolis Millers, who competed in the International Hockey League. The Millers were owned by Ben Berger, seated, front row, and Morris Chalfen.

Minneapolis Mayor and hockey booster P. Kenneth Peterson congratulated Minneapolis Millers' playing coach Ken Yackel in 1961.

At a Crusade for Freedom dinner in Chicago in 1952 were, left to right, Charles Wilson; Henry Ford, national chairman of Crusade for Freedom; Benjamin Berger, Minnesota state chairman, and Admiral H. B. Miller.

Crusade for Freedom raised funds to support the broadcasts of Radio Free Europe to the Communist countries. Ben Berger was one of the nationally-known fund-raising leaders when he posed behind a Radio Free Europe microphone.

During the Cold War of the 1950s, the United States sent balloons aloft to drop propaganda leaflets behind the Iron Curtain. Ben Berger participated in such an effort during a visit to Munich, Germany.

Ben Berger, first president of the Minnesota Prisoners Aid Society, received a service plaque at the organization's annual dinner in 1960. Making the presentation were Nathan Crabtree (left) and Judge James C. Otis.

David Ben-Gurion, first Prime Minister of the State of Israel, met with Mr. and Mrs. Benjamin Berger in 1973. This photo was taken in the library of Ben-Gurion's home in Tel Aviv.

In 1956, Ben Berger and Eric Johnston (left) were among the United States delegation to the first Berlin Film Festival. In the center is Berger's wife, Mildred (Midge).

Left to right, in this 1951 photo, were Ben Berger, Minnesota Governor Luther Youngdahl, and Minneapolis businessman and philanthropist I. S. Joseph.

Hennepin County Sheriff Don Omodt made Ben Berger a Deputy Sheriff at a swearing-in ceremony in 1970.

Benjamin Berger was pleasantly shocked in 1974 when Amicus awarded him a special plaque for inspirational leadership and service. Guest speaker and former United States Attorney General Elliott Richardson made the presentation.

Pictured at the Amicus dinner in 1981 were, left to right, Lloyd Cherne; Warren Spannaus, Minnesota Attorney General; Walter Mondale, former Vice President of the United States, and Benjamin Berger, first president and now chairman of the board of Amicus. (SUN Newspapers photo by Frances Berns).

Midge Berger stepped to the podium at this B'nai B'rith Award Dinner in 1980, when Ben Berger's reminiscences dragged on too long. "You'd better hurry up," she advised him publicly, "because you've been talking for half an hour and you're only up to 1925." Minnesota Governor Al Quie looked on at the left.

It was "a sad day in my life" when Ben Berger sold his beloved Schiek's Restaurant in 1971.

Benjamin N. and Mildred Berger.

The Minneapolis Park and Recreation Board presented a plaque to Midge and Ben Berger after their fountain was finally installed in 1975. The plaque read, "In grateful appreciation for the donation of the Berger Fountain for the citizens of Minneapolis. (Photo reprinted with permission from The Minneapolis Star.)

Ben Berger's son, Lawrence, with his wife, Jackie, and sons William (left) and Robert, came from their home in Honolulu to attend the International B'nai B'rith Humanitarian Award Dinner, which honored Ben and Midge in 1980.

# Chapter Eight

*In 1930, Paramount made me an offer I couldn't refuse for my three theaters in Grand Forks. Thirty-five thousand in cash, plus payment of $1,000 a month for thirty years to lease the Orpheum Theater building, which I also owned and which was not part of the sale. This was wonderful income, especially considering that it was not long after the stock market crash, the cost of living was low, and there was practically no income tax. It was very enticing. I decided to take the deal and move from Grand Forks to Minneapolis.*

*Paramount had been trying to get me out of Grand Forks for years. This was their territory. The movie companies never admitted it publicly, but they had worked up an arrangement among themselves to divide up the country in the 1920s. Each company took an area where it would own theaters—either build them or buy them—without competition from any of the other companies. Twentieth Century-Fox had the West Coast, for example. Paramount had the Upper Midwest.*

There were plenty of squeeze plays in those days. The bigger you were, the harder you could squeeze. That went for exhibitors as well as the studios. The Northwest Theatre Circuit, Incorporated, which was owned by Finkelstein and Ruben, had about one hundred forty theaters. Only one of their houses was in Grand Forks. I had three houses in Grand Forks.

To keep films away from me, Finkelstein and Ruben had bought about two hundred fifty pictures—all of the product supplied by Paramount, First National, Warner Brothers, Fox, and MGM—for their one house. For my three theaters, all that was left was about one hundred fifty films from United Artists, Universal, Pathe, FBO, and Columbia. There was a rule against tying up more films than you could use. In order to get pictures, I had to file a complaint against Finkelstein and Ruben with the Federal Trade Commission in 1928.

But Finkelstein and Ruben got squeezed, too—by Paramount. So did Balaban and Katz, which was an even bigger, a much bigger, exhibitor chain, based in Chicago. Even the biggest exhibitor had to listen when a film company threatened to come into his area and build a real showpiece theater to compete with him. One way or another, motion picture companies got control over exhibiting in their "assigned" areas. I know how that went. I once planned to build a first-run theater on Hennepin Avenue between Fourth and Fifth Streets in Minneapolis, but I changed my mind. I found out that I would have had a lot of trouble buying product for it.

Eventually, Finkelstein and Ruben were pressured out of Grand Forks. Then Paramount went after me, but I gave them a lot of trouble. I made a lot of noise. I was just a little theater owner from Podunk, but I was able to organize other exhibitors to fight the studios, and I got my name into Variety *and all the other trade papers. Once I did that, it didn't matter where I was from. When Paramount saw that they couldn't force me out of business, they decided that they might as well deal with me, make me a good offer, and get me out.*

*I wanted to move my base of operations to Minneapolis anyway. There was more going on there, there were more opportunities. I wasn't getting out of the theater business. In fact, I was expanding. I still had houses in Bemidji and Sioux Falls; then I added theaters in other cities, Fergus Falls, Brainerd, St. Paul, Minneapolis. By the mid-1930s, I had about ten theaters—that was still small potatoes as far as numbers went, but I had a lot of influence in the industry.*

*I was president of Northwest Allied States, which was the predecessor of North Central Allied. On behalf of independent exhibitors, we continued the fight that had begun in North Dakota and a few other places. I sent a monthly newsletter to our members, keeping them informed and keeping their spirits up. I made speeches at various meetings and conventions and was quoted often in the trade press.*

*When Barney Balaban was president of Paramount— he had worked his way up after selling his theater chain to them—I told one meeting that "you can trust Uncle Sam better than you can Uncle Barney." It became a slogan, a rallying cry, for independent exhibitors.*

*I kept punching away at the film companies and at their screwball ideas, like what Abe Montague, general manager of Columbia, told theater owners at a national convention in Milwaukee. He had been writing in trade papers that film companies should get a percentage of theater confection sales—as if the companies weren't getting enough already! Then he went to the theater owners convention in Milwaukee to defend his proposal.*

I hadn't liked the idea in the first place of exhibitors selling candy and popcorn. We were showmen, not popcorn salesmen. But if exhibitors were going to have to sell such items, at least they deserved the profit! So I went to Milwaukee especially to answer Montague. After he outlined his plan, I got up and made a speech ridiculing him. My final statement was, "The only reason Montague didn't ask for the Kotex concession was that he didn't want to be accused of getting blood money."

It wasn't a very delicate thing to say, I know, but the audience broke up. And so did Montague's plan. He never suggested it again.

The longest-running battles with the film industry were over block booking and divorcement. Block booking was when exhibitors were forced to buy a large group of pictures in order to get the ones they really wanted. Sometimes you didn't even get the ones you wanted, even when they were in the contract. I had to sue Columbia in 1937 when they withdrew Lost Horizon from the films I had coming. And divorcement was the word used to describe the effort to prevent companies that produced and distributed motion pictures from also owning theaters.

The first legal action against the restrictive policies of the film industry started in the 1920s in North Dakota. Later, there were suits in Missouri. Eventually the federal Department of Justice got into it and filed indictments against the film companies. Finally there was a consent decree in the late 1940s that block booking was in restraint of trade and that the studios had to sell off their theater chains.

I guess you could say that we won that battle. But the war wasn't over, not by a long shot.

## Chapter Nine

Ben Berger was not always a happy warrior or an accepted leader. Although he believed that he was acting in the best interests of independent exhibitors, some of them thought that his leadership was too divisive, that he was too militant, that he was needlessly antagonizing big studios and thus, in a sense, biting the hand that was feeding the exhibitors.

In Berger's view, timidity was self-defeating. Studios only reacted to extreme countermeasures, he thought; otherwise, they would just chew up independent theater owners and spit them out. So despite periodic flashes of opposition, he continued prodding his fellow exhibitors with the calculated passion of a football coach delivering a pep talk. "Bennie was a master at stirring up the troops," said Stanley Kane.

Sometimes his impetuousness propelled him out on a limb of his own creation. At one meeting, the subject was the high cost of film rentals. Exhibitors were paying a guaranteed price, whether a film made money or not, and there was also an "overage" clause in the event that the film did show a profit. Such demands, Berger burst out in his speech, forced exhibitors to resort to shady means of accounting to film companies so that there wouldn't be any overage—of profit—to report. But when his remarks appeared in print in *Movie Age,* including a quote that some exhibitors "had to be crooks to make a living," Berger backtracked furiously.

The article "was a gross exaggeration, written with the aid of evident straightforward facts but in reality a direct misrepresentation of my standpoint and platform," he said for a subsequent issue of the magazine.

"It has never been my intention to support unfair dealing in business," he continued. "What I have said concerning dishonesty is an actual everyday occurrence in the industry. We all know it but are too secretive to come out with it. But all of this hullabaloo wouldn't get to first base if distributors developed a firm, sound and fair manner of doing business with exhibitors."

\* \* \*

The thankless task of being a lightning rod was not the only concern that occasionally interfered with Berger's state of well-being. There were personal problems as well. Between 1921 and 1934, all of his brothers got out of Poland with money he sent them. Ytzak was the first to come over, followed by the oldest, Sam, then Saul, and finally Lazaar, who had been born after Ben left Poland in 1913. He had only met his youngest brother once, on a trip back to Europe in 1923, so he hardly knew him, and he didn't feel extremely close to the rest of the family, either. "I don't know," he muses. "I hadn't really been raised with them, and I had been on my own and gone for so long."

Still, he felt a familial obligation. When Ytzak arrived in Fargo, Ben tried to help him. The younger brother seemed awkward in the new land, however, as out of place as a canoe in the middle of the ocean. He was experienced at sewing, so Ben found him a job at that, but the two did not have much in common and saw little of each other. Then, in 1922, Ytzak became ill. "I never knew how sick he was," says Ben, who was only twenty-five himself at the time. "Suddenly he was just gone. I don't even know what he died of. If I had had more knowledge or more money, or paid more attention, I probably could have taken him to the Mayo Clinic in Rochester. Maybe I should have. But I didn't feel guilty about it. He had a tough break, that's all."

The memory was not so easy to dismiss, however, nor could Ben overlook another problem in the next few years. His marriage was beginning to fall apart. Buoyed and fascinated by show business in Grand Forks, and occupied with buying theaters in other towns, Berger increasingly found less fulfillment with his wife, Beatrice.

"Our marriage just didn't synchronize," he says. "It just didn't work out."

The atmosphere was not only strained for them, Berger realized, but ultimately would affect their son, Lawrence, born in 1925. Consequently the Bergers separated in 1929. When Ben sold his theaters in Grand Forks and moved to Minneapolis, he went alone, moving into the Radisson Hotel. Later, the couple had a brief reconciliation, which failed permanently in 1932. Beatrice Berger left for Los Angeles. Ben, who had taken up legal residence for a period in Sioux Falls, South Dakota, filed for a divorce, which ultimately was granted in 1934.

He had gone to Sioux Falls to assume management temporarily of his New Granada Theater. The theater, formerly known as the Strand, was a city tradition. It was once considered the show place of Sioux Falls, and its first owner, a man named Jay Dundas, had been classed as the state's leading showman. But independent theaters were unable to compete when Paramount came to town and took over three theaters: the State, the Orpheum, and the Egyptian. The Strand fell on hard times and gradually disintegrated into a ten-cent house.

That did not discourage Berger, who was termed by *Greater Amusements* magazine as "the fighting exhibitor who will take a chance on anything." In 1929, he renovated the Strand from top to bottom. The new interior decor was done to resemble that of a Spanish castle, and Ben installed 850 new seats as well as sound equipment for talking pictures. He also renamed the theater and set a price structure of forty cents tops, to signify that the New Granada was now a first-run house. The gamble worked, except that three years later there were managerial problems, which brought Berger to town to protect his investment.

As it turned out, his sojourn in Sioux Falls had more than business implications. A chance meeting made it a most fortunate episode in terms of the direction it gave his life. He was living in a two-room suite in the Carpenter Hotel, the best hotel in town—Berger enjoyed going first class and, by then, he says, "I was in good shape financially, especially considering that so many others didn't have any money."

The suite was next door to the Democratic party headquarters. "When a visiting party dignitary came to town," says Ben, who was relatively apolitical at the time, "they unloaded him on me for awhile because I had drinks in my apartment."

One day, the dignitary they deposited with Berger for a few hours after lunch was United States Senator Huey Long. Berger and almost everyone else had read all about Long, a well-publicized, colorful, and controversial political character.

Long's nickname was "the Kingfish." He was an advocate of the slogan "every man a king" and of social reforms to benefit poor farmers and workers. Elected governor of Louisiana in 1928, he built roads and hospitals, gave out free schoolbooks, and established night schools for adults who couldn't read. Long had numerous political enemies who were suspicious of his unorthodox methods, and he was accused by the Louisiana House of Representatives of misappropriating state funds, but was later acquitted by the state senate. Elected U.S. Senator in 1930, Huey Long began developing his radical economic plan for a "share the wealth" society, which provided homestead allowances and a minimum annual income for every American family.

Senator Long was as convincing a conversationalist as he was an orator, as dominating in one-to-one settings, slouched in an easy chair and facing his host across a coffee table, as he was in commanding a podium like an evangelistic preacher. Berger, although accustomed to being the center of attention, also knew when it was time to keep quiet. He listened as Huey Long nursed his bourbon and churned out words in a stream of consciousness that seemed to inundate the room.

"Ben, they call me a Communist, but I'm no Communist. I'm nothing of the kind. I just feel that the common people have something to do with creating the wealth and that they should get some of the benefits. Why, look at the secretary of the treasury, Mellon. He's worth eight billion dollars. Do you know how much a billion dollars is?" Now Long was really getting hot. "A dollar a minute from the time of Christ to now—that adds up to a billion dollars. That's just too much power for one man!"

As he went on, it became clear to Ben that Long had no quarrel with private enterprise and initiative. "I'm not trying to stop Andrew Mellon or the Rockefellers from making money," the visitor insisted. But he believed that there should be limits to the accumulation of wealth, that the taxation system and inheritance taxes should ensure equitable distribution to the government and thus, through the government, to the people.

"When Mellon dies, there's no damn reason why all his billions should be left to people who don't deserve it. Suppose he leaves a million dollars apiece to each member of his family. My God, isn't that enough?" he asked rhetorically. "The rest should go to the state so that it can be used for the betterment of working people, used to give them opportunities for schooling and for medical help."

Berger was enthralled, not only by Long's remarks, but by the passion underlying them. "It was one of the most wonderful and enlightening conversations of my life," he recalls.

Perhaps the impressions of the afternoon were further sharpened by the fact that in 1935, while at the height of his fame, and a candidate against Franklin D. Roosevelt for the Democratic nomination for president, Long was assassinated. Had he lived, his impact conceivably could have been eroded with time. Instead, his dramatic and tragic death almost guaranteed that his bold, revolutionary ideas would never be forgotten by those contemporaries with a social conscience, and especially by a Polish immigrant who heard them in his own apartment, face to face, as if from an old friend.

"Besides," says Berger, "when Long was talking about giving money to the people who needed it, I could understand what he meant. When I was a kid, we slept four to a bed. When one of us stretched, another hollered."

\* \* \*

A philosophical framework arose out of that meeting in the Carpenter Hotel, although the foundation had been laid years before. Berger, after all, was no newcomer to the concept of helping one's brother. In addition to literally helping his brothers to a substantial extent, he had been a benefactor for a number of students at the University of North Dakota. While living in Grand Forks, he had started an annual fellowship grant and also had made loans to students numerous times. "But I really never expected to get the money back from these so-called loans," says Berger. "I mentally wrote them off immediately."

He was pleasantly surprised at least once, however. In the late 1920s, a student from Minot named Nate Silverstone came to him for help. The young man's father had died, there were other problems in the family, and he needed $500 for his last year of engineering. Ben gave it to him, learned that he graduated in 1930, but did not hear from the recipient of his generosity for twenty years. Suddenly a letter and a check arrived so unexpectedly that Ben peered at it like an archeologist at an excavation.

"I'm sorry it took so long to pay you back," Silverstone wrote. "Jobs weren't easy to get after graduation and my mother needed my support, and then I went into the army. But I'm glad I can afford to pay you now. I can't tell you how much your help meant to me and to my family."

Without question, Berger found immense gratification in the ability to bankroll the young man from Minot and other such people who, without his assistance, might not have been able to get an education or reach some other worthwhile goal. Money was a tool, Berger felt, not to be worshipped but to be used, applied, enjoyed. There is little opportunity, for example, to pick up a check when dining with Ben Berger. "He rarely even lets me see one," comments his attorney, Sid Feinberg.

An almost comic scene ensued on Ben's second trip back to Poland in 1934. His sister, Mindal, was getting married, and he was paying for the wedding. The custom was to invite relatives to the house for refreshments on the Saturday before the wedding. Roza Berger set the table, putting one cookie at each place.

"Mama," Ben said, coming in and seeing what she was doing, "how come only one cookie?"

"This is the way everybody does it," she replied.

Ben shook his head. "No, just let everyone take as many cookies as they want."

His father, overhearing, was horrified. "Beryl, Beryl, what are you talking about? You can't do that!"

"Why not?"

"Because," Chaim Berger answered, exasperated, "people will fill their pockets with cookies."

Ben laughed. "So what? Let them. I don't care."

The two bickered back and forth until Ben finally settled the matter by saying flatly, "Look, I'm paying for this and that's the way I want it."

Later, they argued over other customs. Each guest was supposed to pay for his own beer, but Ben wanted to pay for all the beer everyone wanted to drink. At the wedding, three musicians were to play. Normally they would get paid with tips from people requesting certain songs. Ben insisted that he would pick up the cost of the music, too.

"Let the people dance for free," he said.

"No!" exploded Chaim Berger.

"Yes!" thundered his son.

Roza Berger merely listened quietly, and probably with a sense of amusement, at this verbal warfare. The clash of wills was just like old times, and she was reasonably certain of the eventual outcome. She was right; Chaim

Berger finally sighed and gave in. He never could reason with his headstrong son.
Ben was adamant, but he also understood his father. They were debating from two different perspectives, two different worlds. The son had broken out of the spending habits of the old world like a fullback bouncing off a pile-up of blockers and tacklers. The father had not. He had been reared in forced frugality and that was the way he had raised his family. Allowing people to take all the cookies they wanted, to drink all the beer they wanted, to dance for free were such astounding concepts that there was no way for him rationally to accept them, even though, thanks to Ben's financial support, the family was living in better circumstances now than when Ben had been a boy.

Yet although he had shaken loose from his father's world, there was a conservative side to Ben, despite his image as an ostentatious spender and inveterate risk-taker. When he owed money, this conservative side showed.

In 1928, he had popped into the First National Bank of Grand Forks to apply for a loan of $30,000—the bank's maximum limit—to buy a theater in Bemidji. For collateral, he offered the theater equipment. How much is the equipment worth, he was asked.

"About seventeen thousand."

"Then," said a somewhat amazed bank president, "how can you expect us to lend you thirty thousand?"

"Because my real collateral is me," answered Berger. "It's my ability to make money."

Even more amazing than the answer, perhaps, was that the bank accepted it and loaned him the money. Berger paid off the debt in about two years. During this period, he had many friends who were investing in the stock market. They urged him to do likewise, but conservatism prevailed and the supposed big spender refused.

"I'm not going to gamble while I still owe the bank," he explained. Years later, he borrowed with no appreciable collateral—this time, the amount was $100,000—from the same bank and paid off the loan in six months. A generation or two has since come and gone at the First National Bank of Grand Forks, but Ben has evidently grown into some sort of legend at the institution. When he returned to the city in 1980 to give a speech to the Kiwanis Club, the time and temperature sign at the bank blinked the message, "Welcome back, Ben Berger."

Berger could be equally circumspect when choosing his philanthropic endeavors. The Jewish Telegraphic Agency once circulated nationally a story it picked up from *The American Jewish World*, the Minneapolis-St. Paul weekly Jewish newspaper. The story was about eighty-six-year-old Harry Goltzman, just returned from a three-week junket to New York, where he saw his eight children for the first time in thirty-four years, and met his eight grandchildren and four great-grandchildren. An unnamed Minneapolis philanthropist, the story related, "made Grandpa Goltzman's trip possible by providing the airplane tickets and traveling money for the aged adventurer."

Berger, who was the "unnamed philanthropist," didn't know about the national coverage until he received a note from Leo Frisch, then owner and publisher of the *American Jewish World*. "You sure made the old man happy," Frisch wrote. "Baron Rothschild of Paris also used to do a lot for people anonymously, so you are in good company."

\* \* \*

There is a difference, of course, between simply donating money, a relatively painless gesture for a person who has it and is willing to part with it, and giving of oneself in addition. Even as a young man, Ben Berger always readily committed himself, particularly when it came to patriotic or veterans' organizations; he was one of the three founders and the first treasurer of the Veterans of Foreign Wars Post in Fargo a few years after World War I, for example. But his acceptance of human obligation became even more pronounced, and his affinity for causes more people-oriented, as he developed roots in Minneapolis in the 1930s and onward. Perhaps it was because of a new maturity. Or because he had more opportunity to exercise responsibility. Or because of the striking impressions left by the meeting with Huey Long. Or because of the thickening pall of despair sweeping like a smog over Europe and threatening, among others, his own family.

Whatever the reason or combination of reasons, the same energy and initiative that had enabled a little theater owner from Podunk to stir up the motion picture industry were put to work with similar startling impact on Minneapolis communal life. Soon after he had come to town, he was approached by two representatives of the community, Ben Friedman and Jack Savlin, who were seeking support for Temple Israel, the Reform synagogue, and Oak Ridge Country Club—this was for Jews, who were restricted from joining other country clubs and golf clubs. Berger wrote out a check for $150 to each, but it was one of the last times he was the solicited party.

Instead, he became the solicitor, the one who approached others. When a cause aroused him, he was the one who roused others. He was a mover and a shaker, a leader, a take charge individual who could make things happen for an organization or a campaign. P. Kenneth Peterson, a former mayor of Minneapolis, who has worked with Berger in aiding ex-prisoners, and who appointed him to chair a Hennepin County committee to improve conditions in the Minneapolis Workhouse, explains his success this way:

"His efforts are genuine and he's aways the same, generous with his time as well as his money. He's willing to champion a cause and delves into it with feelings, dedication, and spirit that few other people have."

Such leadership by example is what impresses Berger's friend from theater days, Martin Lebedoff. "He's a doer," says Lebedoff. "He does more than anyone else, he probably gives more money relative to his own means than anyone else. People know this, they know that he's not in something for his own self-aggrandizement, and they just can't turn him down."

Although Berger is not concerned with personal gain, he is nonetheless fulfilled by organization work and by successful fundraising campaigns. It is as if he finds a mission in life through his ability to generate support for a worthwhile cause—raising $250,000 to build a school for Temple Israel, getting signatures on "freedom scrolls" on behalf of Radio Free Europe, selling Israel Bonds. He delights not only in using his talent unceasingly, but in finding creative new ways of exploiting that talent— "getting an idea" is a Berger specialty.

\* \* \*

One of his favorite organizations has been the Variety Club of the Northwest, consisting of members from show business or associated businesses. The Variety Club of the Northwest is among more than forty similar "tents" or chapters of Variety Clubs International, founded in Pittsburgh in 1928. In order to retain its charter, each tent is obligated to perform a certain amount of charitable work.

The Minneapolis tent was started in 1934 by, among others, theater owners Al Steffes, William A. Elson, Edmond Ruben, A. A. Kaplan and Frank Mantzke, plus W. H. Workman, MGM branch manager, and M. A. Levy, 20th Century-Fox district manager. It indulged in a variety of activities: raising money for displaced persons in Europe and distributing funds through Catholic, Protestant, and Jewish organizations, financing distribution of milk to the needy, assisting the Sister Kenny Polio Foundation. The best-known of its activities came about when Dr. Morse J. Shapiro, a heart specialist, suggested that Variety join with the University of Minnesota in building a hospital for research and treatment of heart ailments. Variety Club members adopted this project so vigorously that it was a grim joke that some of them nearly became the first patients of the now-famous Heart Hospital at the University of Minnesota.

The original four-story facility was opened in 1951. Several additions and improvements followed, including a fifth floor added to the original structure in 1959, a two-story West Wing completed in 1966, and a two-story Cardiovascular Training and Research Center, opened in 1975.

Funds for these and other projects have come from federal grants, contributions through University of Minnesota sources, and continuing efforts on the part of the Variety Club. Through the years, the club has contributed approximately twenty million dollars for various heart hospital facilities, but its efforts would not have been as fruitful—and perhaps not even possible—had not an initial obstacle been overcome. It was necessary to get seed money in order even to begin mammoth fundraising campaigns.

So Ben, who was "chief barker," or president, of Variety in 1952 and 1953, got an idea. What about selling a limited number of tickets, say, 100 tickets at $100 each, and raffling off a new automobile? The car could only be a Cadillac, which was a fixation with Berger. When he had sold his theaters in Grand Forks, he bought his first

Cadillac, a twelve-cylinder model. He paid $5,400 cash for it. It was a symbol of his success, and he has never had any other model of car.

The Variety Club "Cadillac Dinner" was thus born and has become an annual event. Over $200,000 has been raised by the dinner, which now costs $200 per ticket. All 100 tickets are sold every year, thanks mainly to Ben. "He probably sells over fifty percent of them himself," says Lebedoff. Berger, who is still chairman of the event, enters the raffle, too, but after nearly thirty years he has yet to win. Not that he would know what to do with the car if he got it—he probably would donate it to some other charitable cause—but, he says almost wistfully, "It would be nice to win just once." He has come close. One year a ticket came back to him, unsold, just two days before the dinner. Ticket in pocket, he went out for lunch and bumped into Minneapolis financier Irwin Jacobs.

"Aha," Berger thought, "a live customer." He waved the opportunity in Jacobs' face. "How about it? This is the last chance left—I'll buy it if you don't."

"Okay," said Jacobs, "I'll take it."

What he bought, naturally, was the winning ticket.

\* \* \*

If Berger was unlucky at raffles, he could console himself with the fact that he had drawn a winner in another, more important respect: his personal life. Essentially a loner, he had been surprised, following his marital problems and eventual divorce, to find that even a loner could be lonely. After settling in Minneapolis in the early 1930s, he was therefore pleased to reacquaint himself with a slim, vivacious, attractive young lady from St. Paul named Mildred (Midge, to her friends) Goldberg.

They had known each other casually for a number of years because his first wife, Beatrice Gillis, was Midge's cousin. Also, Midge's brother, Sig, managed the World Theater in St. Paul for Ben. Although she and Ben were attracted to each other, it was some time before they became serious. Berger, after all, was not officially divorced until 1934. In addition, there was the potentially awkward situation of his dating a cousin of his former wife. Nor was the courtship aided by his frequent traveling, including the period when he was living in Sioux Falls. Love surmounted all difficulties, however; the two were married October 9, 1935 in the home of her parents, Mayme and Samuel Goldberg.

The new Mrs. Berger had some familiarity with the business world; before their marriage she was a secretary to the sales manager of American Can Company in St. Paul. But that experience was as tranquil as a walk on a summer day compared to the hectic, milti-directional pace of her new husband. It didn't take her long to realize, if she hadn't already suspected it, that keeping up with him would be like running a marathon that never ended. As Berger became an increasingly important public figure with the passing years, there always seemed to be another clash with a movie studio, a new business venture, a continuing need to raise funds for one cause or another.

A wife of less substance and wit might have been intimidated under such circumstances. But Midge Berger is made of stronger stuff. She brought into her marriage a keen perception of her role and of Ben's, of her needs and of his. "There can be only one president in a family," she once commented about Ben's commanding personality and penchant for taking charge in whatever he did. She has never resented his reluctance to share authority; Berger, although willing to listen to others, doesn't make decisions by committee.

"When we have a difference of opinion on something," relates Midge, "one of his favorite responses is to tell me, 'Don't worry, look how well other things have turned out. I must be doing something right.'"

Yet through it all Midge has never lost her own individuality. A widely admired member of the community, she has discovered her own outlets in volunteerism—transcribing textbooks onto tape and recordings for blind people, being president of the local chapter of the National Council of Jewish Women, working for United Jewish Appeal, Hadassah, and B'nai B'rith Women. In fact, she was an equal partner with Ben—they were honored as a couple—in 1980 when they were presented with the International B'nai B'rith Humanitarian Award. It was the first time that a Minnesota couple had been so recognized.

But she has been far more thrilled about her husband's achievements than her own. She takes great pride in the fact that "his accomplishments are especially fantastic, considering where he has come from, his background. He has tremendous drive and will to succeed, is very competitive, and is the most intellectually curious person I have ever known." She also has taken unabashed, star-struck joy in having Hollywood characters such as Gloria Swanson, George Jessel, Roy Rogers, Dale Evans, and Chill Wills in her living room, and in observing the VIP treatment accorded Ben by the movie establishment.

On one of their trips to Europe, the Bergers were met in Paris by a MGM studio limousine, greeted by David Lewis, MGM executive in charge of overseas operations, put up in a suite at the Ritz Hotel, and taken to dinner with a young Hollywood actress and her mother. The actress was Elizabeth Taylor, not long removed from her triumph in the film, *National Velvet*. "She was an exquisite, seventeen-year-old beauty," says Midge, "but I don't think she said two words through the entire evening. Her mother did all the talking."

Midge Berger is not so overawed by her husband that she is unable to puncture the Berger balloon, however. There has always been a healthy, impish quality about her. When Ben was asked by an admirer how he happened to emigrate to Fargo, his wife chimed in, "There was a high tide that day." At the B'nai B'rith Award dinner, Ben's speech about his life story was growing overly long. Midge finally got up from her seat at the head table, walked over to him, and advised him—her voice carrying out over the microphone—that he had better hurry up "because you've already been talking for half an hour and you're only up to 1925."

Berger didn't mind the laugh at his expense, nor does it bother him to be kidded. He even adds to it. "I call her 'dear,' " he grins about his wife. "She calls me names." But he knows that he needs her at his side and he soaks up strength, as if by osmosis, from her moral support and interest in his activities.

"A wife should have as many activities in common with her husband as she can," Midge believes. "Those that she can't join him in, she should be interested in, and he should feel the same way about her activities."

Thus when Berger owned Schiek's Cafe, his wife often ate with him there and learned about the art of wining and dining the public. When he was a member of the Minneapolis Park Board, she used to walk around the lakes of Minneapolis and report to him on the condition of trees. When he owned the Minneapolis Lakers, she even became reasonably knowledgeable about the sport of basketball.

"Which," one wag needled Ben, "was more than you ever were."

# Chapter Ten

In the fall of 1947, Benjamin Berger held a press party to introduce members of his newly formed Minneapolis Lakers professional basketball team. One of the reporters asked him to identify the various players. "I can't," confessed Berger. "I don't know who any of them are. But I know that they're good," he added. The team with which he was not yet familiar—even though he had invested in it—included eventual all-time greats, George Mikan and Jim Pollard. The reporter was somewhat taken aback by Ben's apparently casual attitude toward an investment. Things are not always what they seem, however. This wasn't the first time, nor would it be the last, that Berger had broken new ground, but he hadn't gone into professional basketball without a road map. He knew what he was doing, or at least he made sure others knew what *they* were doing, as evidenced by the fact that the Mikan- and Pollard-led Lakers won the championship six times in the next eight years.

During that period, of course, Berger did acquire more than a passing acquaintanceship with the sport—and with his team. Beyond that, he didn't have to be an expert. Basketball to him was a form of entertainment, of show business, and that was an area in which he *was* an expert. So when the opportunity arose for him to obtain a franchise, the challenge, in his opinion, was no different from exhibiting movies or staging concerts. If there was basic appeal for the public, and the attraction was packaged, presented, and promoted properly, he knew he would sell tickets.

The idea for a team actually started with a young Minneapolis sportswriter, Sid Hartman. Hartman had practically been lifted out of the cradle with the sports bug, and he was bound and determined to get into the newspaper business. By the age of eight, he was a fixture around "newspaper alley" off Fourth Street between Nicollet and Marquette Avenues; the *Minneapolis Times* was on one side of the alley and the *Minneapolis Tribune* was on the other.

He got a job selling newspapers and, when he was sixteen, delivered the *Tribune* to boxes around town. Then Louis Mohs, circulation manager of the *Times* and a friend of sports editor Dick Cullum, suggested that Cullum give Sid a chance as a cub sports reporter. Cullum agreed, since he was short of writers and Hartman was always hanging around, anyway. The salary was only twenty-five dollars every two weeks, but Hartman was ecstatic; he was doing what he loved. Later, when the *Times* ceased publication, he was hired by sports editor Charlie Johnson for the *Tribune*.

Besides being a persistent, tireless reporter, Hartman was also something of a promoter. One day he approached Morris Chalfen, a well-known local entertainment entrepreneur, and suggested that he bring a professional basketball team to Minneapolis. Chalfen advised Hartman to take the idea to Ben Berger, a long-time friend.

Sid followed through. "You know, Bennie," he said when they met, "pro basketball is the coming thing." After receiving assurance from Chalfen that he would join him in any such new venture, Berger's finely tuned business antenna perked up. He didn't have to know much about the sport to realize that it was being played in every school, that there were backboards with hoops on practically every farm, and on garages in practically every city block. That meant the beginning of a built-in audience, if he could give the people the show they wanted to see. "I know the difference between an 'A' and a 'B' picture," was the way he once put it, "and I don't want to have a 'B' picture in basketball."

\* \* \*

Berger and Hartman began plotting. They needed to find a league that would be interested in Minneapolis as a site, and then they needed a franchise. And a coach. And players.

Their first step was to promote an exhibition game between Sheboygan and Oshkosh of the National Basketball League (NBL). This was one of the two principal basketball major leagues of the day—the other was the Basketball Association of America (BAA). The NBL had the better teams, but the BAA had greater long-range potential because more of its franchises were located in large cities, such as New York, Philadelphia, and Boston.

Berger would have preferred to get into the BAA; in fact, at one time he used a contact in the movie business, Joseph Podoloff, to set up a meeting in New York with the movie man's cousin, Maurice Podoloff, who was president of the BAA.

"What about it?" he had asked Maurice Podoloff. "Will you take us in? Minneapolis is a great sports city."

Podoloff shrugged. "Ben, I've got to be honest with you. Your town just wouldn't add anything to our league right now." He hesitated. "Maybe later on," he said, as if trying to put Berger down easy.

The rejection made Berger more determined than ever to compete with the "big towns" some day. But, he realized that he would have to establish a reputation through the NBL first. After the exhibition game between Oshkosh and Sheboygan drew 5,000 fans, the NBL was impressed. So was Berger, who even made "a few hundred dollars" after expecting to suffer a loss; the game, after all, was meaningless as far as who won.

Around that time, the Detroit franchise of the National Basketball League was available, and no wonder. The year before, that team had won four games and lost forty. Berger bought the franchise for $15,000, which got him no players, a few old basketballs, some useless uniforms, and a piece of paper that said that Minneapolis was in the NBL.

Although Berger and Hartman were convinced of the wisdom of the acquisition, others were not so sure. The doubters included members of the press—Sid Hartman's opinion notwithstanding. Berger, knowing that he needed the support of key sports editors and columnists, discussed with them, individually and collectively, his plans to bring professional basketball to Minneapolis. One meeting was in the Variety Club office at the Nicollet Hotel in Minneapolis. Charlie Johnson and Dick Cullum, as well as Hartman, were there. "This is our chance to become major league in sports here," Ben told them, "and I want to be in on the ground floor."

Most newspapermen took a "wait and see" attitude about the merits of the plan, and certainly were not optimistic. Johnson was outspokenly pessimistic. "Bennie, I don't think it will go," he recalls cautioning Berger. "You'll be in a league with a lot of small towns and you'll be competing against University of Minnesota basketball."

"Well, I think the pro game has a great future here and I'm willing to gamble and go ahead," Berger told them. "I hope you boys will cooperate with publicity, beause it will be good for the community."

"Oh, we'll cooperate as much as we can," replied Johnson. "If it's good for the community, we're all for you. But I just hope you don't lose too much money."

\* \* \*

The expenditure for the Detroit franchise was only the beginning, of course. Next Berger needed a coach. His first choice was Joe Hutton, who had had an outstanding winning record at Hamline University in St. Paul. But Hutton eventually declined the offer, even though Berger upped the salary ante three times. The second choice was John Kundla of St. Thomas College, St. Paul, who wasn't much older than the players he would be coaching. As a young man on the rise in his profession, Kundla was concerned about the risks of associating with a new, untried, unproven organization. But Berger offered him a three-year contract and told him, "If this thing doesn't work out, you can go fishing for three years and still get paid." Kundla signed.

As the new organization began putting together its roster, Ben scored a bull's-eye in his campaign to win the respect of the Basketball Association of America. The BAA and National Basketball League were engaged in a bidding war for players. This was long before inflated, modern day salaries, but still the bidding was just as astronomical when measured against other economic standards of that era, and given the fact that the dollar was worth so much more then as compared to today. In fact, both leagues were being hurt so much that the franchise owners called a truce and met in Chicago to see if they could devise a solution to the problem.

Maurice Podoloff presided. "When a college star is graduated," he pointed out, "we are bidding against one another until we have pledged more money than either of our leagues can take in. This will bankrupt all of us." Then he cited as an example "the most extreme case of all. Every team in either league has made a ridiculous offer to Jim Pollard, yet he continues to hold us off and then we go into another round of bidding. And still nobody has been able to sign him."

At this point, Ben Berger stood up and politely waited to be recognized. "Yes, Mr. Berger," Podoloff said impatiently.

"Mr. President," said Ben, restraining a chuckle, "the Minneapolis Lakers have Mr. Pollard under contract." He produced the document and a long, startled silence followed before a chagrined Maurice Podoloff resumed the meeting.

\* \* \*

The man largely responsible for signing Pollard was Sid Hartman, who had a pipeline to his ear through contacts on the West Coast, where Pollard had been playing for the Oakland Bittners in the Amateur Athletic Union league. Hartman also had helped arrange the exhibition game, flown to Detroit for the purchase of that club, aided in negotiations for other players, and done some promotional and publicity work for the Lakers. He had become a twenty-five percent partner in the team not long after its founding.

"The attitude of the newspapers was different then," recalls Hartman, now a nationally known sports columnist with the *Minneapolis Star and Tribune* and also host of his own radio interview show over WCCO. "Today they don't want you involved directly in promoting sports. But back then, before we had major league football, baseball, and hockey, everyone on the staff was trying to do all they could to get a big league team here."

Still, Hartman's role troubled Charlie Johnson, who had become executive sports editor for both of the Cowles-owned papers, the evening *Star*, for which he wrote a column, and the morning *Tribune*. It was one thing, he felt, for the newspaper to promote the Twin Cities as a fertile sports area, to give coverage and to cooperate, as he had promised Berger he would. It was quite another matter, however, to have one of his reporters personally involved with a particular sports organization.

Despite his admiration for Hartman "as a terrific newshound," he couldn't shake his concern that such involvement was wrong. "I thought that it might be a conflict of interest that would hurt the paper," he says. Adding to the dilemma was the fact that Hartman on occasion could be a typical vociferous fan as much as an objective professional. "He would get carried away so much that he would start yelling at the officials," remembers Johnson.

Gideon Seymour, then executive editor of the *Star* and of the *Tribune*, shared Johnson's concern, but he felt that Hartman deserved a chance to control his conduct and to prove that his job performance would not suffer. Sid was eager to be put to the test; certainly he did not want to fumble the journalistic dream realized only a few years before. So a compromise was struck. Hartman would restrain his cheerleading tendencies and he would not cover the Lakers. But he could keep his newspaper job and would not be forced to sever his association with the Minneapolis franchise. That meant that he was pulling double duty—

nights with the *Tribune* and early morning hours at the Lakers office. Hard work and long hours didn't frighten Hartman, however, and they still don't. "I love my work," he says today about his newspaper and radio activities. "I'm at it sixteen to eighteen hours a day. I wouldn't have it any other way."

In addition to Berger and Hartman, there were two other partners. One of them, who had been with Ben since the inception of the pro basketball franchise, was Morris Chalfen, Minneapolis sportsman, promoter, and owner of the Holiday on Ice show. Chalfen was a vice-president of the franchise, with no day-to-day operating role. The other partner was hired to be general manager of the club. He was Max Winter, restaurant owner, former fight manager, sports-expert-around-town, and like Berger, a visionary anxious for a piece of the action from the impending sports boom destined to sweep the country.

Max Winter now heads the Minnesota Vikings professional football team, which he founded in 1961 along with Bill Boyer, H. P. Skoglund, Bernard Ridder, and Ole Haugsrud. Ironically, years earlier, the basketball franchise had been running a contest to choose a nickname for its team. Louis Greene, a copy editor with the *Tribune* and a columnist for the weekly *American Jewish World*, broke a story in his column that the team was going to be named the "Minneapolis Vikings." This premature leak must have created some consternation; at any rate, the basketball "Vikings" suddenly became the basketball "Lakers", leaving the former appellation for Winter to use later when he named his football team.

After the Lakers moved to Los Angeles, someone joked that it was just as well that Greene's piece had forced such a change. Somehow the "Los Angeles Vikings" just wouldn't have sounded right!

* * *

Berger, as was his predilection, was president of the Minneapolis Lakers. If his name, his reputation, his money were on the line, he had to be the final authority. "I have to control my own destiny," he once explained. "One of the reasons I didn't go into the stock market before the depression, when almost everyone else I knew was in it, was because I wouldn't have been in control of what might happen. I felt I should be making money with my own management, not New York stock market management. I would rather trust my own judgment and my ability to make decisions."
This didn't mean that he believed that he knew everything, or could do everything. He recognized his limitations, but he had such confidence in himself that he was restricted most often only by the boundaries of time. If Ben Berger could have been granted a forty-eight-hour day, he might well have taken personal charge of the Lakers. As it was, he realized that he needed a general manager to run the organization on a daily basis.
I went to Max Winter and told him I wanted him as partner," says Berger. "This looks goddamn good,' I told him, 'and you should manage it.' "
Winter, champing at the bit for major league affiliation, agreed. He bought twenty-five percent of the Lakers for $8,000 and assumed operating responsibilities. And therein lay the problem. Berger and Winter were the original two peas in a pod. Both had healthy egos, both enjoyed the limelight, and both wanted to be the boss. Their differences ranged from player deals to the advertising copy for radio commercials. A personality clash was as inevitable as nightfall. Eventually, Berger acquired Winter's interest in the Lakers, and also Hartman's, thus holding seventy-five percent while Chalfen retained the other twenty-five percent.

Unfortunately, the investment was to turn sour although, initially, it had seemed that Charlie Johnson would be wrong about his appraisal of the Lakers' prospects. In its first year, the team won the title, the hearts of the fans, and the attention of Maurice Podoloff. The Basketball Association of America launched a campaign to woo key teams of the National Basketball League. Podoloff himself came to Minneapolis to talk to Berger. "Before, he didn't want us," laughed Berger. "Now he loves us."

Feeling vindicated, and having wanted all along to jump to the BAA and play in places such as New York's Madison Square Garden, Berger was hardly difficult to convince. Minneapolis joined the other league, as did Rochester, Indianapolis, and Fort Wayne, to become part of what eventually would evolve into today's National Basketball Association.

The Lakers continued to win championships, adding players such as Vern Mikkelson, Slater Martin, Bobby Harrison, Herman Schaefer, and Arnie Ferrin through the years. According to Berger, they also were the first team in the league to have a black player, Bob Williams. They were a success at the gate as well as on the court, and by the third season, the club was in the black.

The money-making salad days ended, however, at just about the time Berger acquired majority ownership. Johnson's pessimism was finally justified. Stars such as George Mikan and Jim Pollard retired. The Lakers began to lose. Attendance dropped. On top of these problems, Berger was annoyed and frustrated with the Minneapolis City Council.

One of the credos of show business was to present an attraction in the proper setting. This was as fundamental to sports as it had been to the film industry, when new theaters were built to showcase motion pictures. But Berger was unable to convince the city council that if the Minneapolis Lakers were to be major league, they had to have a major league facility in which to play. The Minneapolis Auditorium, home base of the Lakers, was far from suitable, either in seating capacity or in sight lines. Berger in fact decried the building on plain general principles. "It was inadequate from the very moment it was built twenty-five or so years ago," he said in 1952. "With the growth of the city, and the development of new ventures such as the Lakers, Sportsmen Shows, and circuses, the Auditorium is almost as useless and archaic as the horse and buggy."

The only thing that galled Berger more than having to play in the Auditorium was not being able to play in the Auditorium. Sometimes the Lakers were shut out of the dates they wanted. On one occasion, a Saturday game was scheduled to be televised. This was a big opportunity in those days; the Lakers would have received $5,000 for TV rights. Unfortunately a dental convention was to start the following Monday, and on Saturday when the Lakers were supposed to play, exhibitors had to set up their booths. Berger wanted that TV game—and the national exposure it would bring—so bad that he offered to pay the cost of having the booths set up on Sunday instead. But he was turned down and the game had to be rescheduled for another date.

When the Lakers could not reschedule a game and the Auditorium was unavailable, they were forced to move to the Minneapolis Armory, which was an even worse facility for major league basketball. One year, during the playoffs, both the Auditorium and the Armory were unavailable. So the world champions of professional basketball had to move their play-off games to Hamline University, where only about 2,500 people could watch them play.

Finally, Berger became fed up. "The hell with it," he said to the wall one day.

In 1957, Kansas City interests were after Berger to move the Lakers there. They offered to purchase the club outright or to guarantee Ben enough season ticket sales to pay his expenses. Instead Ben sold the Lakers for $150,000 to a group of Twin City sports boosters headed by Bob Short, owner of a trucking company. He could have gotten more from Kansas City, but he didn't want to be accused of "betraying an obligation to the community just to make a few extra bucks."

The new owners started out optimistically; however, their enthusiasm was soon dissipated as club fortunes continued to sag beneath the pressure of frequent losses and infrequent attendance. About the only person who kept his spirits up was Short. Gradually he began buying out the shares of others, sometimes for ten cents on the dollar, until he acquired control of the team. When it became apparent to Short that the Lakers were not going to survive in Minneapolis, he obtained permission from the National Basketball Association to move the franchise to Los Angeles for the 1960-61 season.

The relocation was like a transfusion. The patient came back to life; Short suddenly found himself with an extremely viable property. In 1965, he sold the Lakers to Jack Kent Cooke for $5 million. It was one of the most dramatic sports ownership overnight success stores of the time, and another chapter was added years later when Jerry Buss bought the team from Cooke for $20 million.

\* \* \*

Benjamin Berger watched these developments with melancholic pangs. He has always regretted giving up the Lakers. "It was one of the worst business decisions of my life," he says. In a curious form of hindsight, he doesn't refer to the decision as a "mistake." A mistake, by Berger's definition, seems to be when a person has all of the information and advice he needs, but does not utilize it intelligently. In the case of the Lakers, "I didn't bother to check the brains of others," he explains, "so what I did wasn't a mistake. It was stupidity."

He violated one of his fundamental rules, which is never to get mad in business. "You can't exercise good judgment and operate smartly if you get mad," he says. When he was managing fighters in Grand Forks, he used to instruct them to rub the nose of their opponent when in a clinch. "I wanted my fighters to get the other guy to lose his temper. I was able to show that if a fighter lost his head in the ring, he would make bad moves and wouldn't be able to do his job."

Berger's bad move came when he blew up at the city council. "I got sore because they weren't cooperating. I thought, 'the hell with you guys, I'll just get rid of this team.' I was *ackshun*, stubborn, about it."

Money was never at the root of Berger's regrets about the Minneapolis Lakers. He didn't begrudge Bob Short his miraculous parlay, even though the $150,000 Ben received was penny-ante stuff compared to the $5 million Short took home. "I didn't care about that," says Ben. "I wasn't in basketball just to make money. I was in it for the challenge and for the pride of ownership."

He says now that his financial losses during the last few years with the Lakers were not so serious that he couldn't afford them. Had he remained owner, it is conceivable, albeit just barely, that the team would have remained in Minneapolis rather than ultimately winding up in Los Angeles. Ironically, Ben could have made his own deal with Los Angeles people, according to Sid Hartman, before the local situation had become critical enough to activate his boiling point in 1957.

"Both Chalfen and Winter wanted to move to California," says Hartman. "They met with Berger at Winter's and Ernie Fliegel's 620 Club restaurant and tried to persuade him to go along. But he wouldn't because he was so civic minded. He wanted the team to stay in Minneapolis." Berger was always proud of the attention and fame the Lakers brought to the city. Well-known New York sportswriters, such as Jimmy Powers and Arthur Dailey, wrote numerous columns about the team. There were features in leading national magazines—*Life, Look, Sport, Colliers, American, True, Newsweek, Time*, and others. In 1954, George Mikan was interviewed by Edward R. Murrow on the award-winning "Person to Person" television show, and many of the Lakers games were telecast nationally.

"It is doubtful if any athletic organization in history has equalled the Lakers' record in bringing publicity to Minneapolis," said chamber of commerce president Gerald R. Moore in 1954.

Berger did not even limit the accolade to "athletic organizations." He felt that "There was no single project ever undertaken here prior to the Lakers which got us more favorable publicity." He cited a trip he took to South America in 1950. "Sportswriters in every country asked me to bring the team there for an exhibition tour."

Having tasted the glory of major league affiliation, Berger missed it—both for himself and for the city of Minneapolis. The city's appetite was ultimately appeased when Calvin Griffith moved the Washington Senators to Minnesota in 1960, followed by the Minnesota Vikings' arrival the next year.

By that time Ben had gotten back into sports, with the Minneapolis Millers minor league hockey team. For several years, he owned the team himself, starting it out of the defunct Denver franchise in 1959. Then Morris Chalfen acquired fifty percent of the stock; he was looking for a tax loss and the Millers seemed to be a likely prospect. It was one of the few times that Berger did not have control of an enterprise in which he was involved. But in continuing as president and decision maker of the club, he was still the "boss."

As he had with the Lakers, Chalfen took a financial rather than a managerial interest. "Now look, Bennie," he said after explaining his reason for buying into the Millers, "just don't get smart and start making money with this thing."

He need not have worried. It would have been very unusual for a community that had become big league in two sports to support a minor league organization in a third sport. The Twin Cities were not that unusual, and neither the Millers nor their arch-rivals in the International Hockey League, the St. Paul Saints, drew enough fans to fill a closet, or so it seemed to the accountants. Despite the tax ramifications, Chalfen was not pleased with the extent of his losses, nor was Berger. In 1964, they closed the doors.

"We couldn't sell the franchise," says Ben. "In fact, we couldn't give it away. So we just walked away from it."

Yet Berger had accomplished a purpose with his gambit. The Twin Cities had been out of professional hockey for about eight years "before I brought it back," he said. "I did it because I wanted to keep us active in the eyes of the National Hockey League. This was the sport of the future in our area, I felt. I thought major league hockey would go over as big or bigger than the Vikings or the Twins."

Berger did not expect—at this stage of his career he did not even wish—to own a team in the NHL himself. It was his hope, however, that his civic efforts would have been recognized, and that he would have had some place, however symbolic, in the organization that eventually founded the Minnesota North Stars in 1967. He was hurt when he was excluded, and it was clear that he had had his last hurrah in professional sports.

Although disappointed, he wasn't bitter. Ben was not inclined to hold a grudge or to dwell on the past. Even though his experiences and associations had not always been satisfactory, neither had they been entirely unsatisfactory. Sports had given him far more good times than bad, and had helped keep him in the news for nearly twenty years. If his day in the spotlight was over, well, he figured, that was show business.

# Chapter Eleven

*Was my involvement with sports worthwhile? I think so. It made me front-page news, a big shot around town. It was a door opener for me—and because of that, other Jews got through the door, too—into Minneapolis service clubs, which until then had discriminated against Jews. Anything that fought anti-Semitism was great as far as I was concerned. If that was all that sports ever did for me, that still made it plenty worthwhile.*

*I knew all about discrimination. I come from a people whose history is saturated with blood. Our blood. I come from a place—Poland—where Jews had to turn the other cheek. From childhood we learned that we had to address every Polish adult—regardless of his or her status—as "Proshe Pana." In English, it meant, "Please, Mister," and in effect it established the Jew as being inferior. We didn't dare argue or fight back about such things or we would have been thrown in jail, or worse.*

*When I came to the United States at the age of sixteen, I was hoping to be through with all that anti-Semitism* stuff. This was supposed to be the land of freedom, the land of opportunity. And it was. Otherwise, people like me would never have been able to do what we did. But that didn't mean that there weren't problems here. Everything wasn't perfect, because human beings aren't perfect.

I ran into anti-Semitism. But at least nobody hit me—and if they had, I could have fought back, and would have. I was in good shape. One thing I learned in the army was the value of calesthenics every day. I kept it up after I was discharged. I developed a regular routine of exercises, which to this day I have continued doing just about every morning in my living room. So I was in good shape, weighed about 148 pounds, and I even used to spar with the fighters I managed in Grand Forks.

But most of the time in my career, I wasn't shown any hostility. I got along. On some occasions I even lived among goyim, in rooming houses where there were no Jews at all. That was a strange feeling for someone coming from a shtetl.

Discrimination wasn't always directed only against the Jews. Blacks and Indians and Catholics were treated something awful. In Grand Forks, I ran into the Ku Klux Klan. It's hard to imagine how strong the Klan was in Grand Forks in the 1920s. Its members were "honorable" businessmen—lawyers, doctors, bankers, salesmen. They elected candidates to the school board and got compulsory bible reading in all public schools. They took charge of city politics, too—one year they had four of the representatives on the five-man commission.

The head of the Klan in Grand Forks was F. Halsey Ambrose. He claimed to be a minister, although he could never show a degree to prove it, and somehow he got himself a congregation of the First Presbyterian Church. Ambrose was a flashy dresser and quite a speaker. He convinced many in his congregation, as well as many others, that "White Protestant Americanism" was being threatened, that the Catholics, who had about twenty percent of the population of Grand Forks, were organizing to take control of the city. Ridiculous.

Ambrose came to talk to me one day at one of my theaters. "What we in the Klan are opposed to," he told me, "are Catholics and niggers." He said he had no quarrel with the Jews, although of course I knew that wasn't true. It was just that I was so well known in town that he couldn't go after me, although I'm sure he would have liked to. But I wasn't in much of a position to argue with him in those days, either.

I did get into an argument later with the Ku Klux Klan in Hallock, Minnesota. The Klan didn't want a Jew operating the theater there. They wanted to run me out of town, so they persuaded the town council to pass a Sunday ordinance law. They knew that no exhibitor could afford to keep the theater going without showing pictures on Sunday, and they thought this ordinance would force me to sell out.

Well, I wasn't going to stand for that. I just closed the house altogether and nobody could do anything about it because I owned the place. That stirred up the Hallock business people. A theater meant a lot to the economy of a small town in those days. It brought a lot of people into town. The businessmen wanted my theater reopened so much that they took up a collection and offered to pay me a month's rent, $125, if I would start showing pictures again. I told them that wasn't necessary, "just get that ordinance repealed." Which they did, Ku Klux Klan or no Ku Klux Klan.

The more I learned about life, and the more I dealt with people, the more I realized how important it was to be *dealing from a position of strength. People respect power. If you have the ability to retaliate, if you can stand up for your rights, you are respected. And you don't have to be tremendously wealthy to fight back and to have influence. I wasn't.*

*The same is true for a country. Even a little country can have influence and make a difference if it's tough enough and determined enough. The State of Israel has made a difference to Jews. It's a homeland, a place to go in case things get rough. As Golda Meir used to say, "Even a stray dog can find a home, so why not the Jews?"*

*Jews have to take care of fellow Jews because the world, until now, has never given a goddamn. The world, or at least the leaders, knew about the crimes being committed against the Jews in Europe, about the gas chambers that were being built, about the ovens in which bodies were burned. There were undergrounds no doubt delivering information to the Pope in Rome, to the Polish government in exile in London, and to the Allies. Yet not a single voice of importance ever spoke out in protest. Not a single country would open its doors to take the Jews in. So six million of my people, one million of them children, went to the slaughterhouse, including my family—my parents, my sisters and their husbands, and my five nieces and nephews, all of whom died in Treblinka.*

*Even as a kid, I was impressed with the problems facing the Jewish people and with how our own homeland could help solve those problems. In Poland, I did a lot of reading about Jewish history. I saw the* pushka, *the little blue and white container, in our home, as it was in almost every other Jewish home. Sometimes there wasn't enough to eat, but my mother always tried to save a* grussian *(a halfpenny) for the* pushka *every day. And she put in another* grussian *in gratitude to God every time my father*

returned home safe from a trip. This money went to Palestine to help buy land and plant trees.
When I got to Minneapolis, I was determined to get involved in Jewish causes. Over the years, I was president of the local Jewish National Fund, which bought land from the Arabs; president of Histadrut, the labor organization; president of the local Zionist organization; and first state chairman of Bonds for Israel. I was also president of the Minneapolis Emergency Committee for Palestine when Israel came into being on May 15, 1948.
My wife and I were once at a meeting in Israel with the prime minister, David Ben-Gurion. The conversation was just small talk, nothing serious, but he did say to us, "It is a pity that people such as you are not living here to help us in our Freedom Fight." But he seemed sort of satisfied when I replied that I considered myself "a soldier for Israel in America."

I didn't see the necessity of all Jews living in Israel any more than all Swedes had to live in Sweden. But I knew there couldn't be an Israel unless Jews in the United States raised money to buy land, build hospitals, help refugees, plant trees. So I've been involved in fundraising drives for those and other causes ever since coming to Minneapolis— there's a forest of 10,000 trees planted in the names of my wife and I in Taron, Israel, and I'm proud of that.

Sometimes, sorry to say, I have called on Jewish people who weren't interested in helping out. Not too many, maybe, but some. They seemed to think that not helping Israel made them more patriotic Americans. But people who can give but who refuse for that reason are just ignorant.

Nobody is a more patriotic American than I am. Nobody loves this country more than I do. But that doesn't mean that you don't fight for what's right. I remember in the late 1930s when I. S. Joseph, a well-known Minneapolis businessman and philanthropist, and I each put up $5,000 to help beat a notorious anti-Semitic United States senator from North Dakota. *There are too many antis in this world, too many people who are against Jews or blacks or Indians or anyone else who is "different." I believe we should fight all of these antis—anti-Semitism and all the rest. I believe that if you have a chance or the ability to correct an evil, you should do it.*

## Chapter Twelve

Hate-mongers abounded in Minneapolis in the 1930s, when the city was infamous as a repository of anti-Semitism. By the late 1940s, the atmosphere had been purified somewhat. Good citizens increasingly recognized prejudice for the evil that it was, and efforts were made to build bridges of understanding between different religions, races, colors, and creeds. Not everyone cared to cross those bridges, of course; for some, hatred was a lifestyle and they merely went underground, becoming covert rather than overt with their feelings.

Stereotypes and mistaken impressions lingered even among people who were not prejudiced, such as Charlie Johnson, executive sports editor of the *Star* and the *Tribune*. "Jews are not joiners," thought Johnson, a past president of Minneapolis Downtown Kiwanis. "They keep pretty much to themselves in their own Standard Club or Oak Ridge Country Club."

It was a prime example of a self-fulfilling prophecy. There had been a longstanding unwritten law among the various Minneapolis service and businessmen's organizations and luncheon clubs, that Jews would not be invited to join. Knowing that they were not wanted and would be stonewalled if they sought membership, they didn't bother to try. Just as the Jewish community built Mount Sinai Hospital in Minneapolis in 1951 because Jewish doctors couldn't get on the staffs of other hospitals, so Jews "kept to themselves" in their own clubs. Therefore, Minneapolis service organizations had no Jewish members. Ergo, Jews were not "joiners."

Such convoluted reasoning fell apart, of course, when subjected to the yardstick of logic and common sense. Johnson began to see the hypocrisy of it all when he was Kiwanis president. "I attended meetings of other groups, including Jewish groups," he recalled. "They kept asking why there were no Jews in Kiwanis and I couldn't explain it. I didn't know." So when his tenure in office was over, he embarked on a personal mission to get the first Jew into Downtown Kiwanis and set an example for other hitherto discriminatory organizations.

In 1951, he found his candidate almost literally right under his nose, or at a nearby table to be more accurate. It was at Schiek's Cafe, which had been a Minneapolis dining institution since 1862.

\* \* \*

Schiek's was a favorite prestigious spot for executives from the media, among other professions. Gideon Seymour, executive editor of the *Star* and the *Tribune*, took staff members there on special occasions.

"Lunch with him meant that the paper was not only going to pop for the lunch but that you were going to get a three dollar and seventy-five cent a week raise," once wrote *Tribune* columnist, Will Jones. "The size of the lunch was supposed to make up for the size of the raise."

The working press enjoyed using Schiek's for interviews when they were on the expense account, and even when working within their own personal limited budgets, there were ways for imaginative newsmen to use the restaurant. Jones told about impressing Harry Reasoner (this was long before Reasoner became a network television personality) by offering to take him to Schiek's for lunch. The key was to "grandly order" for both of them. Jones ordered the chopped liver appetizer, which came in a huge mound, and a mug of dark beer. The chopped liver in the 1940s was twenty cents à la carte, and the beer was fifteen cents, and a free basket of dark bread came with every table. "It was an ample lunch," said Jones, "and for 35 cents apiece it was a helluva bargain, even in those days."

Understandably, the press was nostalgic about the closing of Schiek's in 1971. By that time, the restaurant had moved from 45 South Third Street into the old—1896 vintage—former Farmers and Mechanics Savings Bank building at 115 South Fourth Street. The Third Street building was razed for an urban renewal project; the Sheraton Ritz Hotel was then constructed on that site. Before relocating on Fourth Street in 1961, Berger poured $250,000 into a painstaking renovation of the Farmers and Mechanics building in order to preserve Schiek's image and class. "A visit to Minneapolis without dining at Schiek's," his advertising read, "is like visiting Paris without seeing the Eiffel Tower."

The restaurant's standards must have been maintained; ten years later Berger had paid off all but $9,000 of the $250,000 mortgage. Still, he felt that at age seventy-four it was time for him to get out of the restaurant business, and he was just as nostalgic about it as the press was.

Reviewing the past with Barbara Flanagan of the *Minneapolis Star and Tribune*, Berger remarked that "this is the second time I have had to make a sad business decision. The first was when I sold the Minneapolis Lakers." He pointed to the lobby, where photographs of Fred Schiek, the founder of the restaurant, and his son and successor, Louis Schiek, were on display. "I left a place for my picture to hang after I'm gone. Now, Schiek's is going first. I never thought it would happen this way," he sighed.

As it turned out, news of Schiek's demise was somewhat—if not greatly—exaggerated. Berger sold out to people who attempted to run another type of dining establishment under a different name. They failed. Then, in 1979, he granted rights to the Schiek's name to new owners, and they reopened at the same location and with the same flair, minus only the famous Schiek's Singing Sextette. The city's old-timers, especially, were happy to see the familiar restaurant name in evidence once more.

\* \* \*

Charlie Johnson was among the old-timers who had spent many hours at Schiek's—in his case, when Schiek's was at the South Third Street location. On the occasion in 1951 when he was looking for a Jewish prospect for Kiwanis, the candidate he discovered, of course, was Benjamin Berger. Johnson was eating at the restaurant one evening with his wife and saw Ben and Midge sitting at a nearby table. It was one of those "why didn't I think of him before?" moments.

He walked over, exchanged greetings with the Bergers, and came right to the point: "Ben, how would you like to join my Kiwanis group?"

"I'd love to, Charlie." Then Berger smiled wryly, like a man who knew something the other person did not. "But I don't think you can get me in."

"Why not?"

"Because clubs like yours don't want Jews, that's why not. I went through this with the Lions years ago."
Berger explained that he had been a member—and highly esteemed at that—of the Lions in Grand Forks. This, like Kiwanis and others, was an organization that required prospective members to be invited or sponsored; they could not simply apply to join. So when Berger moved to Minneapolis, the president and secretary of the Grand Forks Lions wrote to the Minneapolis Lions about him. They detailed his accomplishments and concluded that "our loss is your gain."

"Except that I never heard from the Minneapolis Lions," Berger related to Johnson. "They never invited me in. So after awhile, I checked around. There were no Jews in the Minneapolis Club, the Minneapolis Athletic Club, the Auto Club, or in Lions or Kiwanis or Rotary or anything else. I found out that there was a 'deal' to keep us out."

"I understand," Johnson nodded. "I know what you're talking about. But I'm a past president of Kiwanis and I know the score. Let me handle it."

"Well, okay, if you think you can get them to accept me, go ahead and try."

While Johnson was attempting to "handle it," some of Ben's Jewish friends admonished him for his interest in Kiwanis. "They didn't want a Jew before. Now they want you just because the newspapers write about you. Tell them to go to hell," they advised.

"I don't agree," argued Ben. "Jews should be able to join the same organizations as anyone else. But somebody has to start the damn thing. Somebody has to be first."

Things were not unanimous or peaceful over at Kiwanis, either. Johnson and Roy Larson, president of Twin City Federal Savings and Loan Association, were vouching for Ben. Both sponsors were highly respected members of the organization and the community. Still, special measures were called for when considering the unprecedented step of taking in a Jew. A committee of past presidents was formed to discuss the matter and make a recommendation to the board of directors. The discussion took place with some heat at the august Minneapolis Club. "It was a scramble," described Johnson. "There were still some narrow-minded people around." Then a comment was made that caused him to excuse himself from the meeting and telephone Berger at Schiek's. "Something important has come up," he said, "and I can't talk to you about it over the phone. Can I come over now?"

A few minutes later, Berger, to his anger, discovered what that "something important" was. A past president had said he had heard from another party that Berger had been a bootlegger in North Dakota, and according to one story had even served time in prison. "Is that true, Ben?" asked Johnson hesitantly. "If it is, let's just forget about Kiwanis."

Berger was furious with the assault on his reputation. Throughout his life, although he was controversial, he had always been known as an honorable businessman. Even his bitterest of rivals in the motion picture industry had never accused him of skullduggery. He was considered a relentless fighter and tough negotiator who, in the opinion of his opponents, sometimes talked too much and didn't know what he was talking about. But when the dust settled, at least they respected his integrity and, for the most part, admired his determination to protect his rights and those of the "little guy."

\* \* \*

It was true that Berger's belief in individual freedom had on occasion propelled him into conflict with the authorities. He was involved, for example, in an incident in 1927 that could have been the prototype for a modern television comedy skit. At that time North Dakota had a blue law forbidding showing of films on Sunday. But Berger decided he had the right to present a benefit show to raise funds for victims of a flood. No admission was charged, but a collection was taken among the audience. Berger gave the proceeds of over one hundred dollars to J. B. Weineman, district chairman of the Red Cross and also the state's attorney. Weineman accepted the money for the Red Cross and then turned around and charged Ben with violating the law. The court fined him twenty-five dollars.

Censorship was another issue that brought down Berger's hand of wrath—he could have been a spokesman for the American Civil Liberties Union on this subject. He was arrested in 1936 for showing the "sex-dope" picture, *Marihuana*, at his Times Theater, a downtown Minneapolis first-run house located at Eighth and Hennepin. A police matron, Mrs. Blanche Jones, had sworn out a complaint against him after Minneapolis Mayor Thomas Latimer refused to comply with a request from a women's club to stop the movie.

The court case, the first such case in the history of the city, was heard in the municipal courtroom of Judge Vince A. Day. Prosecution witnesses cited allegedly objectionable scenes from the film. Berger's attorney, Sam Halpern, called witnesses who testified that the picture "contained a valuable lesson and was not indecent," and Halpern further argued that "it must be judged as a whole instead of having particular scenes attacked."

If found guilty of showing an obscene film, Ben could have been fined $100, sentenced to thirty days in the workhouse, or both, and his theater license could have been revoked. Fortunately Judge Day found him not guilty. In a written decision handed down after nearly two months of deliberation, the judge declared that a story could be told on the screen without offending decency "even though modesty is shocked by the portrayal." His decision went on to state: "The fact that some of the scenes and language of the picture are coarse and that the plot is cheap and sensational and that the film uses the language of the street rather than that of a scholar does not in itself make it obscene within the law."

Berger could not have agreed more—before, during, or after the confrontation. He never tired of lashing out at the motion picture industry's Production Code Administration; at the Legion of Decency; at movie censors such as Will H. Hayes, Joseph I. Breen, and Eric Johnston; or at any agency or individual with the power to establish what he termed "artificial standards." In an interview in *Variety* in 1954, Berger declared that no group should tell exhibitors what to show in their theaters.

"The public should be the censors—no one group should be," he maintained. "The best censor is the number of tickets people buy to see a picture. If the public wants to see a picture, let them. I am opposed to censorship in all forms."

Although such an opinion, for better or worse, basically prevails today, Berger in his day was known as an extremely controversial figure, not necessarily for his views, but for his outspoken way of expressing them. This, however, was a long way from the accusation or even the suggestion that he had been a criminal, a bootlegger.

Prior to being approached by Johnson, Berger, if not happy about his rejection by the Lions and about the closed society of Minneapolis clubs, still accepted it, at least for the time being, as a fact of life. Nor was he holding his breath about the possibility of joining Kiwanis. But a slur on his honesty was too much. An angry Berger was a sight to behold. Only about five feet, six inches in height, he suddenly seemed to stand ten feet tall. His eyes bulged, and his round face looked like a red ball.

"Listen, Charlie," he exploded, "I didn't give a goddamn before about whether or not I was admitted, but now I want to get to the bottom of this. I want my name cleared."

He suggested in "the strongest possible terms" that Downtown Kiwanis do some checking. "Call the president of Kiwanis in Grand Forks. Call the American Legion— they honored me when I left. Call the Lions Club, or the University of North Dakota or anyone else in town. You'll find out how highly regarded I was. My reputation was one thousand percent."

Johnson, of course, had been more than a little embarrassed about bringing up the remark concerning Ben's background. But the question had to be asked, inasmuch as it had been raised within the committee considering his membership. Now Johnson retreated back to the meeting at the Minneapolis Club, armed with Ben's indignant reaction and fortified by his own determination to break down the discrimination barrier. Two days later, Berger was informed of his acceptance as a Kiwanian and the walls indeed did start tumbling down; today, minorities are no longer a rarity in any Minneapolis service organization.

\* \* \*

Although the circumstances leading to Ben's induction into Kiwanis were somewhat touchy, he joined with good grace. It was not in him to remain bitter; he did not even regard the Lions with any particular rancor. In fact, around the time he became a Kiwanian, he was invited to speak to a local Lions chapter. The invitation came because of his status in the community; the club had no idea of what he was going to say or about the affront rendered by an earlier generaton of its membership.

"I told them, though," grinned Berger. "I told them about the letter from Grand Forks and the invitation that never came from Minneapolis. I told them that Jews were citizens just like everyone else and were entitled to the same benefits. I reminded them that anti-Semites are the children or grandchildren or whatever of immigrants, too, and these immigrants, just like me and other Jews, came over here to find freedom."

There was, as Berger recalls, "a little squirming in the crowd" as he delivered his message. "They really did feel terrible and afterward wanted me to become a member." He might have accepted, had not Kiwanis been in the picture, but now he declined graciously. "I'm not blaming you people," he told the Lions. "It wasn't your generation that did it. I realize what the situation was in this town."

Naturally Kiwanis is the service organization for which Berger holds the most affection. He appreciated what it did for him and other Jews, and he wanted to return the favor. A plan solidified in his mind, and one day in 1979 he bumped into Charlie Johnson about a week before the next meeting.

"Are you going to be there Tuesday?" Ben asked.

"I'm not planning to. There's a Minnesota Vikings luncheon that day."

"Charlie, do me a favor and attend." They were standing on the mezzanine floor of the Leamington Hotel. Ben looked around him conspiratorially, like a little boy who can't hold a secret any longer but doesn't want anyone else to overhear. Then he whispered, "I'm going to announce a gift of $100,000 to the Kiwanis Foundation, for programs and scholarships for poor kids."

Johnson stared in surprise. "For crying out loud," he chuckled. "I just came out of the Foundation office after giving them two stocks worth $600 and here you come with $100,000. Okay, don't worry. I'll be there."

As part of the announcement ceremony, Ben had an opportunity to retell the story of how he happened to join Kiwanis. "You could have heard a pin drop," said Johnson. The story was old hat for some; perhaps, for some, it didn't change their ideas this time any more than it had before. But many in the new generation of members were hearing for the first time about a facet of anti-Semitism nurtured by service organizations.

"I had a feeling that his speech woke up people who never realized that there was such a problem," says Sid Feinberg, one of the Jewish members of Kiwanis. "They left with the thought, 'By God, Ben is absolutely right. It's a shame that it was ever that way.'"

If so, Berger may have struck another blow in the battle to prevent it from ever being "that way" again. Beyond that, his donation underscored his belief in the responsibilities of those with financial means equal to, or in many instances much greater than, his.

"All my life," he said, "I have wondered what I could do to make a better tomorrow. Maybe this money can give a lot of people a lot of better tomorrows."

## *Chapter Thirteen*

The snub from the Lions wasn't the only sore spot that festered for many years in the hide of Benjamin Berger. Something else had been bothering him for at least as long, if not longer. Almost from the time that sound came to motion pictures and his theaters started playing the talkies, Berger could never understand why the American Society of Composers, Authors, and Publishers (ASCAP) was entitled to royalties from music contained in a film.

The author of the book from which the screenplay was written didn't get paid every time the film was shown in a theater, Ben told himself. Then why did he, as an exhibitor, have to pay for songs that were sung or played? As early as 1930, when he was president of what was then known as the Northwest Theater Owners Association, he had progressed from muttering silent protests to actually attempting to organize an army of rebellion.

"Something that the independent exhibitors must get rid of is the so-called music tax," he said in a president's newsletter, dated January 16, 1931. "That's an out and out holdup, protected by the law, which can only be done away with through organization."

Of course at that time, and for years afterward, no one accepted Berger's proposition that ASCAP could be defied. Other exhibitors were no happier than he was about the music tax, but it seemed perfectly obvious to them that nothing could be done about it. If Bennie wanted to rant and rave, let him. The odds against a little theater owner from the Midwest successfully challenging ASCAP bordered on the preposterous, and Berger's unique ability to "rally the troops" did not extend to involving them in kamikaze missions.

Admittedly, even Berger would have viewed his chances as a very long shot, had he stopped to think about it. On the other hand, his entire business career had been a long shot. What would the odds have been against an immigrant, a Polish Jew, becoming the dominant entertainment entrepreneur of a town in North Dakota controlled by the Ku Klux Klan? Berger was never shaken, swayed, or awed by obstacles or by the Establishment; to him they merely represented temporary inconveniences that could be overcome as soon as he figured out the best way to go around them.

\* \* \*

Early in his business career as a confectionery store owner in Fargo, Berger fought a battle in court for the first time. His landlord had raised the store rent but softened the blow by promising Berger that he could stay in the building for at least another year. Then the landlord reneged and tried to evict him. Berger said no, on the grounds that he had a verbal contract.

In court, a witness claimed to have had a conversation in which Berger said he was going to move out of the store.

This of course would have meant that Berger himself did not intend to live up to the contract.

"Hey," Ben whispered in protest to his attorney, Harry Lashkowitz, "I not only never said I wanted to move, I never even saw that fellow before."

"Okay," said Lashkowitz quietly. "Let's see if I can trip him up."

In his cross examination, he proceeded to fire a rapid series of questions requiring simple yes answers. Then he closed the trap: "And were you told to say that Mr. Berger said he wanted to move?"

"Yes," responded the witness, before realizing what he had just admitted.

Case closed. Obstacle overcome.

When Berger operated the Orpheum Theater in Grand Forks, he wanted to put movie advertising in the windows of an adjacent store with a common wall. The store was part of the theater building complex and the common wall had windows that faced into the theater lobby. The building was owned by twelve partners, eleven of whom lived out of town. The twelfth, who managed the property, was not too kindly disposed toward Jews in general, and Berger in particular. He refused to allow him to advertise in the windows and ignored his offer to buy the building.

Ben got the names and addresses of the absentee owners from a friend and assistant cashier at his bank. One by one, he wrote them and concluded an agreement to buy their shares. He didn't have the money himself, but he had worked out a deal with the bank for a loan. As each partner sent in his stock, it went directly to the bank as collateral. The remaining owner lost the fight before he even knew the bell had rung; control of the building was jerked from beneath him and he, too, finally agreed to sell his shares. Another obstacle overcome.

Berger also was more than willing to challenge established industry giants. In 1933 he was sued by Electrical Research Products, Inc. (ERPI), a subsidiary of Western Electric, which was owned by American Telephone and Telegraph. Early in the history of the talkies, ERPI was an exclusive supplier of theater sound systems. Berger, having no choice, bought ERPI equipment when installing sound in his Elko Theater in Bemidji, Minnesota. He paid $18,000 for the equipment and also had to agree to a service charge of $20 a week for eight years. After two years, however, he decided that he was being charged for maintenance that he didn't want, didn't need, and wasn't getting; the sound system seldom required attention and what little it did require was rendered by his projectionist.

"I do not wish to have service from you," he informed ERPI. "Therefore please discontinue the weekly fee."

The supplier refused, stating that the weekly fee was part of the purchase contract. When Berger disagreed, ERPI sued for its equipment, won, and took it back, leaving Ben out $18,000. By that time, other sound systems were available. He equipped his theater with Ultraphone, manufactured by a Minneapolis businessman and friend, Joseph A. Numero, and then sued ERPI for his original $18,000 plus an additional $30,000 in damages. The grounds included an unfair attempt to claim control over sound equipment and parts; violation of interstate commerce laws, because exhibitors were not allowed to use competitive parts in servicing ERPI equipment, and violation of the Sherman Anti-Trust Act. In addition, Berger contended that he had purchased—not leased—the equipment, and therefore ERPI could not claim possession of it.

The trial took place in Bemidji and lasted one week, after which the case was taken under advisement. While the judge was considering his verdict, Electrical Research executives decided that if they lost the case, it would set a precedent that might result in thousands of other exhibitors throughout the United States voiding their contracts and filing suit. Before the judge's decision was handed down, therefore, they made Berger a cash offer that more than covered his time, trouble, and the costs of the ERPI and Ultraphone systems.

"Thank you," he said, accepting the settlement.

Another confrontation with powerful industry names occurred when Berger bought the Lyceum Theater in Duluth from Minnesota Amusement Company. He discovered that he could not get good pictures for it. So he filed a $1.3 million antitrust suit in federal court in Minneapolis against Paramount, Columbia, Loew's, RKO Radio, 20th Century-Fox, United Artists, Universal Film Exchanges, Warner Brothers, and Minnesota Amusement Company. The complaint charged a conspiracy to fix the length of movie runs and minimum admission price terms, to discriminate with respect to licenses granted independent theater owners, and otherwise "to restrain and monopolize the motion picture business." The case never went to trial. Two of the defendants, Columbia and RKO, were able to wriggle away because they had consistently supplied product to the Granada, an independent theater in Duluth. But the other seven were ordered to answer twenty-three of the twenty-five specific charges. Their lawyers then quickly got together with Berger's counsel, made out-of-court cash settlements, and agreed that the Lyceum would get second-run exhibiting privileges.

Berger, who came from a country where there was little freedom and justice for the defenseless, was overjoyed to be in a place where the legal system was an equalizer. He never hesitated to use the system as a club with which to pummel and humble the most powerful.

\* \* \*

In addition to legal persuasion, Berger used politicking as a weapon against those who, in his view, wanted to crush independent businessmen. In 1947 he spearheaded a campaign against the movie industry on behalf of the North Central Allied Theater Owners Association. He threatened to take out a full page advertisement in a Washington, D.C. newspaper to publicize the "inequitable manner" in which film rental prices were fixed, and to urge "President Truman and Congress to probe the entire motion picture industry."

The threat had teeth, because federal intervention was a concept that the studios and their distributors abhorred; for that matter, so did many exhibitors, Berger among them. "Neither I nor the NCA board of directors want government control or intervention," he said. "But we prefer it to having the 'little fellow,' the small town or small suburban theater owner, trampled under by the industry's policy makers."

The ad, which had been set in type, was never run. Berger agreed to kill it in return for an agreement by film companies to "honestly and sincerely" study the NCA complaints. "Now we are getting somewhere," he commented. "Local distributor representatives are well aware of the precarious position of the small exhibitor, but the top people in Hollywood might not be familiar with the conditions that have brought about our complaints. But if they were made aware of these conditions, I think they would change them, because we can prove that small towns cannot make money under present high film rentals."

His triumph was short-lived, however. Even after film companies studied the complaints and were "made aware" of the conditions, their conclusions still put them on the opposite side of the fence from Ben Berger. There were no perceptible improvements and there was no relief in sight as far as his angry eye could discern. So through the years he continued to harangue, cajole, badger, and beg Washington for help.

The pressure he and a few others exerted finally began to squeeze out some response. In 1955, the chairman of the Senate Small Business Subcommittee agreed to hold hearings prior to possible introduction of legislation to control film prices. The chairman was a man Ben knew well. He was Senator Hubert H. Humphrey of Minnesota.

Humphrey and Berger had been friends for more than ten years. Their relationship had started through Midge Berger. She came home one day stimulated by a study class on international relations, sponsored by the National Council of Jewish Women. The guest lecturer had been, in Midge's words, "a brilliant young man," Hubert Humphrey, who was then a teacher at Macalester College.

Soon afterward, Humphrey went into politics, and Midge reminded her husband that this was the young man who had so impressed her. Humphrey ran for mayor of Minneapolis in 1943, lost, and then helped form Minnesota's Democratic-Farmer-Labor party in 1944. With the aid of that vigorous new coalition, he was able to win the mayoralty race in 1945. A dauntless crusader, he quickly established a reputation nationally as well as locally as a liberal firebrand; he was elected to the United States Senate in 1948 and that year led the fight at the Democratic National Convention for a strong party stand on civil rights.

Throughout this period and later, Berger supported Humphrey, both financially and as a friend. On election night, 1948, there were only two other couples at the Humphrey home with Hubert and Muriel, listening to returns over the radio. They were Ben and Midge Berger, and Hennepin County Sheriff Ed Ryan and his wife.

\* \* \*

That Ben should have been so close to a liberal crusader was both understandable and astonishing. He was as staunch a Republican—"my Republican friend," Humphrey used to call him—as Hubert was a fervent Democrat. Ben's belief in private enterprise was as firmly cemented as was the Democratic party bedrock of public controls manifested through the government. Whereas Humphrey for most of his political years had the admiration and support of the unions, Ben was forever squabbling with union leaders over those elements of the labor movement that he felt interfered with his rights as an individual businessman. One of these was the practice in the amusement industry of featherbedding: paying wages to musicians who didn't play, or to motion picture operators who weren't needed, or to stagehands when there was no stage scenery to move.

"Who absorbs the costs of featherbedding?" he once responded in an interview. "The public. Who do you think? When the price of steel goes up, you pay more for a car. It's the same in my business. When exhibitor or promoter costs go up, you pay more for tickets."

In Broadway stage circles, the story was often told of Charles Laughton supposedly playing the trombone in a five-second sequence of *Major Barbara*. Actually Laughton merely simulated a performance and music came from a recording. But the producers of the play had to pay $628.51 a week to four "standby" musicians who sat in the wings while Laughton went through the performance sequence. "Some people call this featherbedding," said Berger, "but I call it racketeering. It's just the old clip game."

When Berger owned the Lyceum Theater on Eleventh Street in Minneapolis, where Orchestra Hall is now located, he promoted live concerts and stage plays on occasion. He was constantly battling with the stagehands union and with the musicians union. One time a dramatic actress did not want an orchestra to accompany her act, but the union insisted that Berger had to hire local musicians, anyway. He argued, but to no avail.

"So I took these musicians and had them play in the anteroom to the ladies' restroom," he recalls. It was small consolation since he had to pay them, but at least his action, in his words, "told them what I thought of them."

Despite their philosophical differences, however, Hubert Humphrey and Ben Berger enjoyed a rapport, which evolved out of their mutual fundamental concern and compassion for people, all people. "All people" included the Jewish people. "I think I had something to do with teaching Hubert about the suffering of the Jews," says Ben, and indeed, throughout his career Humphrey was considered a friend of Israel and of American Jews, and was supported by them.

Humphrey and Berger both clearly saw the need to help and protect the common man. The former visualized such help as coming through federal government channels; his friend felt that individuals—such as himself—should exercise a significant share of the responsibility.

"There is a certain special mentality for earning a lot of money," he points out. "If you take an average 1,000 people, give them $1,000 each, and put them someplace for a year, two or three guys will probably wind up with ninety percent of that money. But if they can do it, more power to them, as long as they operate within the boundaries of human decency and in some way recognize their obligations to society."

He doesn't completely oppose government programs. "Social security, workmen's compensation, unemployment benefits, health benefits—these are examples of government help, but the government is able to help by getting money for such programs from people who amass wealth." Thus Berger, a man of above average means, has never objected to being heavily taxed. Yet he also sees merit in a taxation system that allows wealthy individuals to set up scholarship programs or foundations, thereby encouraging them to share their good fortune.

"I have always paid my stagehands and projectionists as much as possible," he says, "but these are not high paying jobs. Yet in the 1950s the son of one of those employees was graduated from law school. That wouldn't have been likely thirty years before. It became possible when people such as my employee's son could get scholarships for higher education."

He sees himself as a proud capitalist, and he believes that "the United States has the best form of government in the world." Parenthetically, he predicts that communism ultimately will fail "because human desires are unstoppable. Where there is no private ownership, there will never be pride of ownership, and people will never stop striving for something of their own. They must have incentives; without incentives, there can be no progress." So he will brook no interference with the rights of the individual to succeed and to enjoy that pride of ownership, whether the interference comes from giant government, giant business, or giant labor.

Of course one man's interference might be considered another man's salvation. But though Hubert Humphrey traveled a different road in attempting to meet the needs of the people and solve the problems of the world, he still understood where Ben Berger was coming from and that didn't diminish Humphrey's affection and respect for him.

Hubert was able laughingly to overlook the "misguided impressions" of his Republican friend—those matters about which they disagreed—because the matters about which they agreed were far more important. Humphrey was the son of a South Dakota druggist driven into bankruptcy by the Depression, and so he, too, was concerned about the welfare of the small businessman. Humphrey, too, loved his country. And if he did not personally feel the magnitude of pain from the lessons of the Holocaust as did someone whose family was murdered by the Nazis, he nevertheless grasped the effects that history had had on the Jewish perspective.

\* \* \*

When, in Berger's opinion, small theater owners needed relief from the "evil men" of Hollywood, it was as natural for him to turn to Senator Humphrey for help as it had been for the anxious Humphrey to have a friend at his side while awaiting the senatorial election returns of 1948. The movie industry was well aware of Berger's close relationship with Humphrey, and they feared its consequences. As the threats of federal intervention mounted in the mid-1950s, with hearings finally scheduled to begin early in 1956, so did the fury of industry counterattacks.

A column in the *Hollywood Reporter* took great pains to point out that "on this trick that's to come up before the Senate small business sub-committee, it might be well to set up the fact that Senator Humphrey, who is chairman of that sub-committee, is from Minnesota and Bennie Berger, who always has been one of the chief agitators against anything and everything the major distributors do, is also from Minnesota."

The column went on: "Berger, by the way, is a rich man. He made it all out of exhibiting motion pictures. He's one of those 'crying millionaires' that have wept themselves into sacks full of picture money, none of whom have a leg to stand on in their beef against picture companies. No picture company ever walked away getting the best of a transaction with Berger."

*Variety* wrote that the film companies "are reportedly considering presentation of evidence that the hearings were not inspired by the majority in exhibition but by a small group of chronic dissidents. This approach, if adopted, would further attempt to prove that those who were instrumental in bringing about the investigation are not the true spokesmen of the theatermen."

To Berger, such attacks were a transparent smokescreen. He shrugged them off like a bear that didn't feel like playing with her cubs. He had never disputed the fact that he had made money in exhibiting. But in his opinion, many smaller, less sophisticated exhibitors were not able or allowed to make money and were afraid to speak out. It was these theatermen who deserved protection against gouging, thus requiring "chronic dissidents" to speak for them.

Humphrey, meanwhile, was determined not to let his association with Berger tarnish his approach to the hearings. He told *Variety* that he and the committee were carefully avoiding "any prejudgement of the issues to be presented at the hearing and we do not entertain any preconceived notions of the ultimate facts to be established. The sole purpose of the undertaking will be to try to resolve problems which may be shown to exist between distributors and motion picture exhibitors, many of whom are small, independent businessmen."

In retrospect, it was an unusually august body that conducted the hearings. Serving with Humphrey, who some day would be vice-president of the United States and later a presidential nominee, were two other Democrats—John F. Kennedy of Massachusetts, destined to be president four years later, and Wayne Morse of Oregon; plus two Republicans—Barry Goldwater of Arizona, an eventual nominee for president, and Andrew Schoeppel from Kansas.

After the hue and cry surrounding the investigation was over and all of the various representatives of film companies, exhibitor organizations, and government had been heard, the aftermath was like a Super Bowl letdown. Nothing much happened. By midsummer, the prestigious committee issued a ninety-one-page report, which recognized the problems, suggested arbitration, and made other general recommendations, but did not provide small-town theater owners with any relief from what Berger insisted were unfair film rental prices. His hope for legislation that would transform the film industry into some form of public utility was shattered, and he was bitterly disappointed.

"This is a disheartening body blow," he said. "I just feel that the committee failed to understand and did not get to the meat of the problem." A year later, he resigned as president of the North Central Allied Theater Owners. His battles with the film industry would continue, but in the future he would be waging them more as an individual speaking for himself rather than as a representative of an organization.

"I know that I have been criticized because of my militancy, and that is one of the reasons I think it is time for me to step out," he explained. "I call a spade a spade and I may not be tactful or diplomatic, but that's my nature. And I believe I have made an honest effort to be fair and to fight for the exhibitors at a cost to me personally."

\* \* \*

There is no question that, throughout the years, Berger took personal gambles in espousal of his principles. Normally, however, the price he paid was more mentally wearying than financially costly. In his lawsuits against film companies, or his experience with the Lakers, or his involvement in Schiek's, or any of his other wide-ranging ventures, the material risk was not terrifying. He never liked to be wrong or to lose, but if it happened, there was always another day. With one exception. That was in connection with his decision to challenge ASCAP and once and for all rid himself of a practice that deeply offended his sense of justice. This was one match that he literally could not afford to lose, and yet the outcome on the face of it seemed almost inevitable.

The powerful Society of Composers, Authors, and Publishers—the "American" part of the name came later— had been founded in 1914 by composer Victor Herbert and a group of associates. Through this organization, members were able to collect fees for public performance or distribution of their works. Initially, fees were earned primarily through sales of sheet music (a favorite form of family recreation at that time was to gather around the piano for singalongs). A new and sizeable source of revenue was added in 1923, when ASCAP won a suit against WOR Radio, a station in Newark, New Jersey. After that, radio stations were required to pay an annual fee to ASCAP for rights to play music created by Society members.

The evolution of talking motion pictures was another bonanza for ASCAP. Since music was now being heard in movie theaters, exhibitors were charged a music tax. The cost was based on variables such as the number of seats in the theater and the size of the town, and was deliberately scaled low—sometimes as little as twenty or twenty-five dollars a year—so as not to overburden the exhibitor.

Still, Ben Berger was infuriated with the thought of having to pay any sum, however small, for what he believed was an unreasonable demand by the power structure. For more than ten years, he wrote fiery letters and delivered blistering speeches, attempting to mobilize exhibitor support against the music tax.

"It's a matter of principle," he explained to Stanley Kane, executive director of North Central Allied.

"I understand that," said Kane. Inwardly, though, he questioned whether the campaign would ever change ASCAP's mind.

Berger had similar doubts, but he was determined to keep trying. He decided, "I have another way that I'm going to fight them."

"How?"

"I'm going to stop sending them their goddamn fee, that's how."

In 1941, he ceased making payments. The daring revolutionary gambit dispatched shock waves through the ASCAP offices in New York. This, after all, was no paltry matter. There were approximately fifteen thousand theaters in the United States; even with many of them paying only token fees, ASCAP was collecting $5 million annually. But if one exhibitor could simply stop paying, so could all the others.

The organization reacted to the possibility of losing this revenue like a man having his pocket picked. It reasoned with Berger and scolded him. It contacted him personally and through third parties. It sent statements and letters and registered letters, but the flow of correspondence was strictly one way. Berger blithely ignored the communications as if they were presented in a foreign language. After five years of being spurned like a jilted suitor, ASCAP decided it was time to get serious, and legal action was instituted in federal court in Minneapolis.

During the period when Ben had been refusing to pay the fees, he owned fifteen theaters. The law provided for a fine of $250 to $10,000 every time a movie was shown by an exhibitor without an ASCAP license. Ben's total chain of theaters played films roughly thirty times a day, which meant that he had accumulated thirty violations a day for five years. It was obvious that, even with a conservative fine, he would be bankrupt if he lost. It was like a man risking all he owned with one roll of the dice at the craps table, except that winning would only entitle him to walk away with no more than what he had when he started.

The gamble made sense only to Berger. "I'm going to stick to my guns," he snapped. "I'm right and ASCAP is wrong."

Other independent theater owners applauded Ben's courage, although privately they may have questioned his sanity. They did promise a measure of financial support. Kane had secured approval of a resolution that each exhibitor would contribute the equivalent of one year's ASCAP fee to help Ben pay his legal expenses.

"But Bennie, you're still their sacrificial lamb, you know," said Kane.

"Yes, it's my neck that's on the block, not theirs." As resolute as he was, even Ben Berger was entitled to some moments of uncertainty. "They must be tickled to death that they got a shmo to do what I'm doing."

The case was heard in the U.S. District Court of Judge Gunnar H. Nordbye. From the outset the pressure on Berger was cruel. Even the ASCAP lawyers seemed to feel sorry for him. On the third day of the trial he was visited in his office by the opposition chief counsel.

"Ben, let's stop this now," the lawyer argued. "Please. You're going to lose. You don't have a chance."

"Then what do you want? Why are you here?"

"We don't want this. We don't need it. Listen," the lawyer leaned forward beseechingly, "I'll tell you what we'll do. We'll cancel the charges against you and you can write your own ticket on future agreements. We'll give you a new license and you pay anything you want, whatever you feel is right."

Under other circumstances, Berger would have been suspicious of such an offer. It could have been coming from a lawyer who was merely trying to ease his own client out of an untenable position. But not this time. Berger's instinct told him that the overture was sincere. Moreover, from a practical standpoint, he had already admitted—although only to himself—that he was risking much too much, for much too little. Yet his concept of justice and his sense of independence would not permit him to back down.

"No," he told the attorney, "I can't do it. You were wrong yesterday, you're wrong today, and you're going to be wrong tomorrow. I'm going to win."

On September 9, 1948, Judge Nordbye issued his decision. In a seventeen-page memorandum that stunned the amusement industry, he declared that the ASCAP fee was illegal and uncollectible, and he ruled against the plaintiff's request for damages and against their request for an injunction to prevent future violations of their copyrights.

"Sound for pictures cannot be played unless the music included in the sound track is also played, in that dialogue and music are on the sound track and obviously cannot be separated," wrote Nordbye. "It is estimated that eighty percent of the music used in films is copyrighted by ASCAP members."

The judge therefore pointed out that ASCAP potentially could deny any theater owner the right to carry on his business "because without the right to exhibit films containing ASCAP music, no theater owner would be able to stay in business. It would be possible to refuse a theater a license or to impose an exorbitant license fee which can sound the death knell of every motion picture theater in

America." To grant relief to the plaintiffs, Nordbye ruled, "would extend their copyrights in a monopolistic control beyond proper scope." Public interests consequently transcended music copyrights as applied to motion picture exhibiting.

The improbable had happened. The underdog, Berger the giant killer, had won. No longer would he or any other theater owner have to pay the music tax that he had been fighting for nearly twenty years.

# Chapter Fourteen

*I was named exhibitor of the year by Allied States Association as a result of winning the ASCAP lawsuit. Years later, I got the Trueman T. Rembusch Award from the National Independent Theater Exhibitors Association for: "defending the rights of all exhibitors, having the confidence of those with whom he works, being diligent in pursuit of goals and considering only the good of the whole with little or no regard for himself."*

About the only thing I didn't get from exhibitors was all the money I was supposed to have coming to pay for my legal fees. After the lawsuit, Stan Kane told them, "Okay boys, now is the day of reckoning," and he asked them to contribute what they had promised. Many of them did—about ten thousand dollars came in—but that still left about ten thousand that I paid out of my pocket. But that was okay. I didn't go through all that with reimbursement on my mind, and I wasn't going to worry about who came through with his contribution and who didn't.

I'm not a worrier about much of anything. Maybe I was a little concerned about how the ASCAP thing would come out, but once I decided to go ahead I was determined to keep going, whatever it took. I know a lot of people thought I was cuckoo, and I might have been a little cocky about it, but it was my decision and mine alone. The only people I really discussed it with were my attorneys, Sam Halpern and Lou Schwartz. They felt that our case was similar to the ethyl gas case, where ethyl manufacturers were denied the right to require that filling stations buy licenses to add tetraethyl lead to gasoline. I didn't think I needed an ASCAP license any more than a gas station needed an ethyl license, and I was right.

Right or wrong, it doesn't pay to waste time regretting past decisions. What's done is done, and I don't carry my troubles with me. My wife and I have done a lot of traveling—we've visited nearly ninety countries—and when we leave I leave my business behind. I never wanted to get any calls from the office, except in an absolute emergency. I got a letter once a week letting me know what was going on, but I didn't want to hear about any bad news. I hired good people and I expected them to take care of any problems. My philosophy was: If there's a robbery, call the police department. If there's a fire, call the fire department, don't call me.

Of course, occasionally I had to step in after getting back. While we were in Hawaii in 1949, Schiek's was contacted by lawyers representing the musical, Oklahoma, which our Sextette was performing at the restaurant. Because of the way we were advertising the name of the musical and the way we were presenting it, the lawyers threatened to get an injunction to stop us.

When I got back and found out what was going on, I decided that I didn't want to pay any more legal fees on this one. So I went to New York myself to talk to the counsel

representing the musical. "What's this all about?" I asked him. "We're just singing your show's songs and we're paying ASCAP for that."
"Well, you're doing more than that," he said. "You're using the name, Oklahoma, in a way you shouldn't be, and you've got your people in costume."
"All right, look," I answered. "What do you want? What will be kosher?"
"First, don't have someone start off your show by explaining the play."
"Fine. We'll do away with that."
"And don't say that you're putting on the musical, Oklahoma. Don't advertise that way."
"All right. We'll just advertise 'Songs from Oklahoma.' "
Then the lawyer said, "We don't want your people in costume, either."

The discussion had been going great up to that point, but when he said that, I had to tell him to hold on a minute. I couldn't agree to that without consulting my attorney. So we talked for awhile. He knew me because he had been with the Hays office, the office that censored movies, and he knew I was okay, although I seldom if ever agreed with the Hays office. Anyway, I don't think the Oklahoma people wanted to make this any more of a big deal than I did, and as long as I gave in on all the other points they decided to let our Sextette continue to do our show in costume.

See, I could compromise. In fact, one year Andy Smith, general sales manager of 20th Century-Fox, and I worked out a conciliation plan that could have been a model for the entire industry to follow in mediating differences between distributors and exhibitors. Smith had written to me after reading in the trade press that I was encouraging lawsuits by exhibitors. He suggested a roundtable discussion before any more lawsuits were filed. He hoped that the industry—or at least his company—could find a way other than legal action to solve grievances. That was fine with me—it was what I had been looking for. I invited him to Minneapolis to discuss what was known as the Minneapolis Mediation Plan. The plan, which was adopted, created a special North Central Allied grievance committee consisting of E. L. Peaslee of Stillwater, and Henry Greene, Jr. and Ted Mann of Minneapolis. The purpose of the committee was to hear complaints that any exhibitor in the Minneapolis area had against 20th Century-Fox. If grievances seemed to be justified, they were referred to another committee, this one set up by Fox.

I felt that if both sides handled their end in a spirit of fair-mindedness and open-mindedness and made every effort to dispose of disputes in an amicable manner, we could eliminate ninety-nine percent of possible litigation with Fox. A trade magazine even ran an editorial cartoon coining a name for the idea. The "Smithberger."

I wish I could say that the Smithberger solved everything and that all of the exhibitor organizations and all of the film companies got together. But it didn't, and they didn't and eventually the idea fell apart. Maybe it would have worked if everyone had tried harder.

I learned a long time ago that you really have to be committed if you want to accomplish something. Nothing happens in this world unless you make it happen. I've been committed to a lot of things that have given me a lot of pleasure and satisfaction. Not all of them were in business. In fact, the more successful I was in business, the more influence I had and the more I was able to accomplish outside of business. It wasn't just a case of giving money— it was making a commitment to do something worthwhile.

One of the areas that gave me the greatest satisfaction was prison reform. Talk about helping people who can't help themselves. There are few people who fit that category more than prisoners. I know. In 1952, I was appointed by Minnesota Governor C. Elmer Anderson to the twelve-person Citizens Advisory Committee on Penal Reform. In 1957, I became the first president of the Minnesota Prisoners Aid Society, which had been formed through the efforts of another organization, the American Association of University Women. Later, I suggested that the state of Minnesota employ an ombudsman, which it has done since 1972. We were the first state in the country to have such a person. After we started it, other states joined us, including Michigan, Kansas, Oregon, Iowa and Nebraska. I also was a member of the Adult Corrections Commission, the parole board, from 1966 to 1974.

Often I was asked why I was willing to spend so much time in the field of corrections. I didn't have to find words myself to answer that question. Those I was able to help answered for me. I remember getting a Christmas card from one prisoner. "Mr. Berger," he wrote, "hundreds of inmates are going to bed at night with a prayer on their lips for you." Another time, a woman told me, "I light a candle every Sunday for what you have done for my son in prison." Money can't buy the kind of feeling I got from hearing those kinds of words.

Even though as a layman I had a lot of experience and was able to use my common sense in dealing with and trying to solve problems, there was one problem that was particularly difficult for me to understand. It was the Minnesota law stating that a person sentenced to life imprisonment for first- or second-degree murder could not be released by the parole board.

## Thank You, America 179

*I'm not saying that there aren't people who don't deserve to stay in prison. But I thought that the whole idea was to rehabilitate the convict. When someone shows that he is no longer a menace to society, he should be released after a period of time and become a taxpayer, instead of living on the taxpayers' money.*

I first became acquainted with the problem when I was on the Citizens Advisory Committee on Penal Reform. I was vice chairman of the committee. The chairman was Henry M. Gallagher of Waseca, who had been chief justice of the Minnesota Supreme Court from 1937 to 1944. Gallagher had wanted me to be chairman, but I declined. I felt that he was more knowledgeable and qualified.

The committee conducted investigations of penal institutions for one year. As part of the investigations, Henry Gallagher and I were granted the right to receive uncensored letters of complaint from inmates. I received the bulk of the letters, responded to each one, and also visited each of the complainants in prison. I always wanted to check out the situation personally and also wanted to make sure there was no retaliation against the writer of the letter.

One of the letters came from a convicted murderer named Joe Redenbaugh, who had been in prison since May 1917, and was asking for help in getting out. Redenbaugh was only nineteen years old when he was sentenced to life imprisonment; the newspapers called him "the toughest kid in America."

Redenbaugh's case interested me above all others. There was no father in the home where he grew up, in Lincoln, Nebraska, and his mother took up with other men and she beat him. He quit school while in the fourth grade. But later in prison, tests showed that he had an I.Q. of over 150. He became a model inmate, following up on his *education through correspondence courses and eventually getting an engineering degree from the University of Minnesota. He even got a job offer for $18,000 a year—a very good salary by standards of that day—from Boeing Aircraft in Seattle.*

*I felt that Redenbaugh should no longer be in the institution. This was consistent with my philosophy that an inmate who was completely rehabilitated should no longer be a ward of the state; he should be paying taxes to the state. It was when I tried to do something for Redenbaugh in the mid-1950s that I learned that, under Minnesota law, lifers could not come before the parole board. The only way they could be released was through the pardon board, consisting of the governor, the attorney general, and the chief justice of the supreme court.*

*I proceeded to file an application on behalf of Redenbaugh. I then appeared before the pardon board to argue his case and presented a letter from Boeing with their offer of a position. At the conclusion of my argument, a response was made by Chief Justice Roger Dell. We knew each other pretty well. I ran into him a lot because of my prison work, and he was also my landlord. He owned the building that housed my theater in Fergus Falls.*

*Dell said, "There's no question about this man's guilt. He killed a woman and a policeman, he pled guilty, and he was given life."*

*I answered, "A man sentenced to fifty years can be paroled someday, but if he's sentenced to life he's there for the rest of his days. But what if he's changed? Doesn't that count?" I asked.*

*"Life means life," replied Dell.*

*I was amazed by his nonchalance and shocked at the lack of human feeling. "So does that mean that even if he is rehabilitated, the only way he can come out is in a box?"*

*Thank You, America* 181

"Use your own words," he told me.
Well, that really bothered me. I checked into the pardon board and found that no lifer had much of a chance with that body. It was almost impossible to get out. There were fewer lifers, percentage-wise, released in the state of Minnesota than in any other state in the Union.
So I called a special board meeting of the Minnesota Prisoners Aid Society. I told them what had happened and said that the reason I took the presidency of the organization was because I thought we should try to change anything that was wrong in the area of corrections. I urged that we go to the legislature and get a law passed allowing lifers to appear before the parole board.
The Society board accepted that idea and was able to interest a state senator in proposing such a bill. Eventually the bill passed, with the provision added that a lifer must remain in prison for twenty-five years, less time off for good behavior—which meant a minimum of seventeen years. After that time, if he was no longer a menace to society he would be released.
Within a short time after the law went into effect in 1962, all of the more than one hundred lifers in Minnesota prisons, including Joe Redenbaugh, were released. There hasn't been a single recidivist among them.
I'm proud of that fact, and I'm proud of the law, which was my brainchild. It's something for which I hope to be remembered.

## Chapter Fifteen

In the 1950s and early 1960s, there were, as there are now, varying philosophical approaches to the subject of prisons and their occupants. Some people in the field of criminal justice—lay people as well as professionals—viewed imprisonment as measured punishment for wrongful acts. Others saw it as a time for rehabilitation, since most of the people who were in prison would eventually be out, rubbing shoulders again with the rest of society. Some were concerned about giving too many privileges to prisoners, while others were concerned about giving too few. To some, the increasing crime rate indicated the need for a "get tough" policy and to others it indicated a need to find the causes of crime.

Yet the issues were not so sharply drawn as to put people squarely and irrevocably on one side or the other. Depending on varying situations and inmates, it was possible at certain times to believe in punishing and on other occasions to believe in rehabilitating. It was also possible to be angry both at the criminals and at the conditions that made them criminals. In other words, the problem was extremely complicated, involving not only lifers such as Joe Redenbaugh, but the the entire criminal justice system, and no one was more aware of the interwoven complexities than two Minneapolis lawyers, P. Kenneth Peterson and Neil A. Riley.

Paul Kenneth Peterson, born in 1915, was voted "Outstanding Young Man in Minneapolis" in 1949 by the Jaycees, and was also named one of the "100 Leaders of Tomorrow" by *Time* Magazine. Starting in 1948, he served four consecutive two-year terms in the Minnesota State Legislature, and later he was twice elected mayor of Minneapolis.

While in the legislature, he was chairman of the Civil Administration Committee, which dealt with all state agencies and boards, including the parole board. From 1965 to 1967, he was president of the Minnesota Prisoners Aid Society, an organization formed in 1957 with the aid of a $40,000 donation from Benjamin Berger to finance the first two years of operation.

Impetus for the organization came initially from a study by the Minnesota branch of the American Association of University Women. The study showed that it cost (at that time) $135 a year per inmate for adequate parole supervision as compared to $1,100 per year to keep the same person in prison. Thus the Minnesota Prisoners Aid Society wanted to encourage discharge of deserving inmates. Among the organization's goals were to offer work programs to train inmates prior to their discharge and job assistance programs to help them after their release from prison. "We want to put the emphasis in the future on the rehabilitative rather than the punitive aspects of penology," said Berger.

Although Peterson thinks that "if you have a man bent on crime, he should be kept in prison," he has always believed that there is a "fair percentage of people who are capable of being rehabilitated." With steadily rising costs, this was a viable consideration. "You can now send a kid to Harvard for what it takes to keep him in prison," he once pointed out. Ultimately, he himself was involved in helping to decide the release fate of prisoners. In 1973, Governor Wendell Anderson appointed him to a five-year term with the Minnesota Corrections Authority, a new name for the parole board.

However, by 1973, being a member of the board had become a full-time occupation, and it was more than Peterson had bargained for. "You didn't give me an appointment," he half-joked with Anderson. "You gave me a sentence, and I'm going to parole myself." He resigned in 1974 to accept a position as a federal administrative law judge.

Neil Riley is a contemporary of Peterson's, one year younger, and has been a judge since 1964, first with the Hennepin County Municipal Court and then with district court. Riley has a droll sense of humor. When *Minneapolis Star* reporter Abe Altrowitz asked him for personal information in order to prepare a standing story in the event of Riley's death (a standard newspaper practice with well-known people) Riley began his response by quipping, "I just can't wait to see this in print."

Riley was vitally interested in the circumstances leading to lawbreaking. "Two-thirds of crime is probably committed when people are on alcohol or drugs," he said. Altrowitz's "obituary" about him reflected this interest. "He was one of the leaders in the move to change drunkenness from a crime to an ailment, handling 'drunks' as patients instead of malefactors," wrote Altrowitz, using the past tense, of course, because his subject at this point was supposed to have just died!

"He served as chairman of the Minneapolis Task Force on Homeless Alcoholics. He was a member of the Governor's Commission on Law Enforcement, serving on the subcommittee for reform of criminal law. He was a member of the Minnesota State Judicial Council, the Hennepin County Task Force on Alcoholism and Inebriety and the Advisory Board of the Catholic Welfare Services of Minneapolis."

No discourse on Riley would be complete, however, without reference to his involvement in an organization formed to deal with prisoners on a personal, one-to-one basis. "He was the founder of Amicus," reported Altrowitz, "which was designed to help convicts make such adjustments on being released that they wouldn't gravitate towards another crime and a return to prison. He founded Amicus with the financial help of Benjamin Berger, Minneapolis theaterman and park commissioner."

\* \* \*

Riley and Berger, who was president of Amicus for three years and is now chairman of the board, had joined forces like two commanding generals using their combined might in an effort to destroy the enemy. Berger was looking for a new crusade to replace his once-pet project, the Minnesota Prisoners Aid Society, which had essentially sputtered to a stop, changed its name, and become more of a "think tank" in the area of criminal justice. Riley had long since concluded, by the time he met Ben in 1967, that the "Amicus way" offered the best hope for reducing the rate of recidivism. Today, he is still adamant about the needs of ex-convicts.

"We lock people up and they haven't been so secure since they left the womb," he says. "Then we slip them back into the community jobless, friendless, penniless, scared to death. They are not better equipped to compete but rather less equipped. A person has to have a job when he gets out and he has to have a meaningful relationship with another human being who cares whether he lives or dies."

In his opinion, the "meaningful relationship" is impossible through the parole officer system. "The professional has nothing to offer," he says. "First, he's tied up with paperwork. Second, the prisoner is not going to go back to his parole officer for help over the bumps. He's not going to tell the P.O. what he's doing wrong. You don't tell that to your jailer. The prisoner is afraid that 'if I tell you I'm back on the sauce, you'll revoke me and I'll have to go back to the joint.' "

In Riley's opinion, the solution is therefore to use compassionate volunteers, and Amicus tries particularly hard to convince ex-offenders to work with the newly paroled: "They know more than a Ph.D. about the problems the parolee is going to have. Helping the just-released prisoner gives these volunteers a feeling that there was a reason for all the suffering they themselves went through."

Not all of the Amicus volunteers who work directly with the parolees are former prisoners themselves. But all of them—at least the successful ones—share the ability to relate to the mental anguish of the parolee. For that kind of assignment, Neil Riley oddly enough would not consider Ben Berger a desirable volunteer, despite Ben's deep concern and powerful motivation to aid fellow human beings. In this instance, Ben's determination and knack for overcoming adversity are considered a disadvantage—he is too much of an achiever. Even with an occasional slip along the way, he has been too successful against adversity.

According to Riley, Amicus volunteers have to understand failure. Riley has heard professionals in the criminal justice system fall back on the axiom, "try, try again and you will succeed." But to an ex-con, "that is a crock," he says. Consequently, the organization selects workers carefully, properly and—judging by results—effectively. Although exact statistics are unavailable and Amicus claims no specific rate of success, indications are that only about twenty percent of its parolees return to prison, as compared to seventy percent across the board in the United States.

The rejection, if one could call it that, of Berger as a "desirable volunteer" in no way diminishes the total and undisguised admiration that Neil Riley has for him. "My impression of Ben is one of sheer astonishment," he says. "People who know in the Jewish community say that he gives more of his personal finances proportionately than anyone else. He's one of the great givers, but that doesn't mean that he has anywhere near the wealth you might think by what he's giving away." To those who criticize Berger's ego, Riley responds, "I wish all people of means had that ego. And his is understandable. He's self-made and entitled to be proud of what he has accomplished."

Berger's generosity is not the only facet of his character that amazes Riley. There is also his willingness to put trust on the line and to accept the hazards of a decision with remarkable equanimity. Ben and a Minneapolis businessman named Arthur Stillman were among the handful of Twin Cities employers who were willing to give or find jobs for convicts. Berger employed them at his theaters and at Schiek's Cafe. "He's something of an ex-officio housemother for paroled convicts," was the way *Minneapolis Star* columnist Jim Klobuchar once described him.

The trust misfired on occasion, and never with more certainty than the weekend that burglars broke into Schiek's. Ironically, Berger got the news Monday morning while getting ready to attend a parole board meeting. Evidently someone had hidden in the basement after the restaurant closed Saturday night, and had let the others in after the cleanup man left early Sunday morning. The intruders hauled away the safe, plus seventy-eight pounds of steer tenderloin from the freezer. To add insult to injury, they had made themselves at home while "working," as evidenced by the crumbs and opened bottles left behind. The thieves had taken a large cut of ham from the freezer and apparently had prepared sandwiches, eaten at the front bar, and quenched their thirst with bourbon, gin, and ale.

Klobuchar translated the incident into an entertaining column. There were grounds for suspicion, he wrote, "that the boys were on familiar terrain." The grounds included the fact that Berger had had two safes in the basement, one with cash and the other with nothing in it. The thieves did not make the mistake of taking the wrong safe!

To Riley, the incident is further proof of Berger's capacity to rebound in extraordinary circumstances. Schiek's was probably "knocked off" with the inside help of a con Berger had befriended and employed. As Riley points out, it is normal for a person to have difficulty exuding good will after becoming the victim of a crime. "But not so with Ben. He was unperturbed. The Old and New Testaments talk about 'loving thy neighbor.' But we don't. Except for Ben. He, so help me, really does love his neighbor."

\* \* \*

Berger brought the same outlook into the criminal justice field (which he has been known to call the "criminal injustice field") as he did to his other endeavors. He was dedicated to protecting the rights of the individual. "These people are criminals," he said of inmates. "They have been convicted and have been sentenced for their crimes. But they are also human beings and should be treated humanely."

When he was a member of the citizens advisory committee investigating conditions in Minnesota's penal institutions, Berger was visibly disturbed over what he believed was unjust treatment of prisoners. He therefore propelled himself into the investigations with such vigor and passion that he soon became the committee's dominant figure, even though he lacked the professional credentials of the prestigious committee chairman, former Chief Justice Henry Gallagher.

It was a classic example of the impact that could be made by a nonprofessional. "Laymen such as Ben absolutely have a place in the field of corrections," said P. Kenneth Peterson, who was a member of the legislature at the time. "They add common sense and practical experience. In Ben's case, over a long period of years he has acquired an invaluable understanding of human behavior."

Berger understood, for example, that prison riots were often born out of a series of nagging incidents and complaints, which individually might be insignificant but which collectively, over a period of time, could turn an institution into a pressure cooker. "Inmates don't riot to get out of prison," he said. "They riot to call attention to conditions inside the prison." After demonstrations at Stillwater State Penitentiary in 1953, Ben got into a verbal sparring match with Jarle Leirfallon, state commissioner of public welfare, who lashed out at him for saying that he could see "some justification for strikes and riots which have taken place in penal institutions."

"That is a careless and foolish statement," charged Leirfallon. "Berger is inserting into this picture a most dangerous concept. Prisoners can never take power into their own hands. I don't want prisoners, businessmen, legislators or anyone else to get the idea that prisoners have the right to riot."

Although Berger doubtless could have chosen his words more carefully, it was also probably true that the commissioner misinterpreted, whether deliberately or not, the meaning of the remarks. Berger did not choose to carry on a feud in the newspapers, but he did set the record straight in a letter to Leirfallon.

"Of course I am opposed to riots, inside institutions or outside," he said. "I feel, however, that I know human nature. When human beings are pressed as hard and as bad as they were at Stillwater, they are bound eventually to blow their top. You know that inmates get time off for good behavior. When they blow up, thereby canceling their good behavior time, the situation must be pretty bad."

To ease the tension, Berger became the unofficial trouble-shooter of the penal reform committee. He made frequent visits to institutions at Stillwater, St. Cloud, and Shakopee, checking complaints and discussing suggestions from inmates and staff. The inmates were startled to meet someone from the outside who not only was sincerely interested in listening to them, but who could also get action.

One of the first complaints he heard at Stillwater was that the coffee tasted "lousy." Berger tried it himself, agreed with the appraisal, and took a sample to a St. Paul laboratory for analysis. Armed with the analytical report, he then went to the state purchasing department, where it was discovered that the coffee did not meet the specifications set up at the time of purchase. Suppliers were getting paid for a grade of coffee far superior to what they were actually delivering. The "honest mistake" was quickly rectified.

There were other examples of insensitive treatment or of needlessly irritating procedues at state penal institutions that Berger and the penal reform committee brought to light. At meals, food was being deposited in one large bowl, which meant that meat, potatoes, vegetables, and dessert became one sloppy stew. Why couldn't meals at least be served in the type of compartmentalized mess trays that the military used, Berger wondered? They could, and subsequently were. Lights were being turned out at 9:15 P.M. "Why is that?" Berger stormed. "These men aren't children. Why have them sit in the dark so early and brood?" So a change was made to lights out at 11:00 P.M. Prisoners complained about lack of screens, which allowed hordes of mosquitoes to invade their cells in the summer, about being allowed to shower only once a week, about infrequent uniform changes and little or no washing of uniforms. These, too, were areas in which the committee was responsible for significant improvements.

A number of inmate grievances were uncovered as a result of a recommendation by Berger, adopted by the penal reform committee and approved by Governor C. Elmer Anderson, that inmates be allowed to send uncensored mail to the committee. "I want to find out what makes Sammy run," explained Berger, borrowing from the title of Budd Schulberg's novel, "and I don't want a guided tour. I want to get the inmates' point of view." He maintained that the freedom to write letters "will be a safety valve for them. It will give them a chance to get things off their chests, to appeal, to give us their view of what's going on without fear of retaliation by the guards or by the administration. Then we can check the veracity of what they say and take necessary action."

The letters were to be sent to Berger or to Henry Gallagher. But Berger did not see any notice about the new policy in the *Stillwater Mirror*, the prison newspaper, and after about four weeks neither he nor Gallagher had received any correspondence from Stillwater.

Ben found it difficult to believe that not a single convict at Stillwater had any complaints. He, Gallagher, and the secretary of the penal reform committee, James Otis, who was later to become a state supreme court justice, met with Governor Anderson and Leirfallon. "I thought that we got the okay to let prisoners write us," Berger said. "No letter has come from Stillwater."

"Warden Utecht has been informed," replied Anderson. "I wrote him authorizing it."

"Well, nothing is happening." Berger was aggravated. He suspected that Utecht resented the committee and that the warden believed the committee was interfering with his prerogatives. "Now the question is," Ben told Anderson, "who is the boss, you or the warden?" He and his two associates added that unless the question was satisfactorily answered and the letter writing policy instituted on behalf of the inmates, the penal reform committee would resign.

The meeting provided the governor with the impetus and inspiration to quickly resolve the matter of who was "the boss," and mail from convicts began to arrive by the basketfuls. The apparent personality clash and power struggle between Berger and Utecht continued, however. When Ben visited the prison hospital one morning, a patient told him that he couldn't get any books from the prison library. Other inmates in the ward confirmed his contention.

"You can't get anything to read while you're in the hospital?" Berger was shocked and mystified. "Why not?"

The prisoner shook his head. "They just won't let us."

At noon, Berger met with the warden, who said simply, "They're lying." Well, that was possible, Ben thought. There were plenty of liars in the penitentiary. But he decided to check further, which he had freedom to do because he was authorized by the governor to go wherever

he wanted in the prison. He met with the librarian and with hospital guards, and found to his complete satisfaction, or dissatisfaction, that the inmates were correct. They couldn't get books from the library.
"Warden, you told me they lied," he said, back in Utecht's office. "But that isn't true."
"I thought it was," replied Utecht. "There was a rule against getting books but I issued an order to change that rule two years ago."
Berger was skeptical about the explanation. But, not wishing to antagonize the warden and become embroiled in an argument, he let the matter pass. The important thing was that books suddenly became available to the hospital section of the prison. The ability to get action like this soon earned Berger the trust and respect of the inmates.
From other quarters, however, it attracted a certain degree of wrath. One time Midge, Ben's wife, took a call at home. "If Berger doesn't lay off of Utecht," a voice warned, "something is going to happen to him."
Ben told Gallagher about the call so that the citizens advisory committee would be aware "just in case something did happen." Otherwise, he ignored the threat, and never did stop applying pressure to get fair treatment for inmates. But he did talk to Warden Utecht soon afterward. "I didn't tell him about the call," he says, "although it made me mad and it shook up my wife pretty bad. What I did tell him was that I wasn't after his job. 'I wouldn't want your job for a hundred thousand dollars,' I said. 'I just want to humanize this institution and rehabilitate people.' "
Berger never wavered when it came to the goal and principle of rehabilitation. Anything was possible, he thought in his prison reforming days. Just look at Joseph Redenbaugh, formerly labeled "the toughest kid in America." He had educated himself in prison, and he now had a

standing job offer from Boeing at a salary rivalling that of most of his civilian contemporaries. Who could deny how this man had changed!

\* \* \*

Early in his life, at about the age of twelve, Joe Redenbaugh had known what his goal was—he wanted to be a thief. His ambition was to be the best thief possible and to pursue his career "honorably" by never betraying or stealing from another thief, which wasn't at all incongruous for a boy who considered thievery an honorable profession.

By his teenage years, Joe was a confirmed criminal who had served time in jail. Eventually, he wound up in St. Paul, driving a stolen car. A policeman stopped him. Joe shot and killed the policeman, although maintaining later that the gun had gone off accidentally. A few days after this tragic episode, Joe and a friend carried out a murder contract on a woman named Alice Dunn. They had been hired by her husband, who paid them $2,000. After the murder, Redenbaugh ran away to San Francisco to hide out, but was caught soon afterward. He was returned to St. Paul for trial, sentenced to life, and taken to Stillwater Prison.

In the penitentiary, the maladjusted, untrained human failure somehow pulled his act together. Joseph Redenbaugh had always had native intelligence, but no one had ever pointed him in the right direction, much less provided him with an ordered structure of priorities. So it remained for Redenbaugh himself to draw on a rare capacity for introspection and analysis. He extracted strength from incarceration, rather than drowning in despair, and utilized his lonely cell as a command post of personal development.

He completed one correspondence course after another, enroute to a high school degree and then to his

University of Minnesota engineering degree. Gradually it dawned on the prison staff and population that a mechanical genius was in their midst. When there was a problem with the heating system, the warden, Douglas Rigg, asked Redenbaugh if he could help. Redenbaugh made some equipment design changes that solved the problem and saved the state approximately ten thousand dollars in maintenance expenses.

Initially, Joseph Redenbaugh had been as resigned as a person could be to a lifetime behind bars. Slowly, however, he changed from his own description of himself as "a dumb punk kid who didn't know anything." As he matured and acquired a delicious new sense of self-esteem and values, he began to dream haltingly of a new start. That dream brought him into contact with Ben Berger.

\* \* \*

The law preventing lifers from being paroled was unjust, as far as Ben was concerned, and he was determined to do something about it, both on his own and as a member of the Minnesota Prisoners Aid Society. "Any law made by man can be changed by man," he has been fond of saying all of his adult life.

When Berger was a member of the Metropolitan Airports Commission (MAC), while perusing the financial statement, he found to his astonishment that MAC funds were being kept in a savings bank. They were drawing four and a half percent interest, whereas certificates of deposit were paying up to twelve percent at the time.

"What the hell!" expostulated Berger. "We're losing a lot of money here. Why are we keeping that money in a savings account?"

"We have to," explained the MAC attorney. "It's the law. We would have to get the approval of the legislature to do anything different."

"Well," Berger answered without hesitation, "why don't we just do that!" He proposed a resolution that the attorney contact the legislature to seek a new law that would allow the commission to invest its funds more intelligently. The resolution passed, appropriate contacts were made, and, as a result, the law was changed in 1975. Since then, according to MAC executive director, Raymond Glumack, "we have earned literally millions of dollars more than we would have otherwise, thanks to Ben."

Berger was equally impatient with the rule regarding lifers. He discovered that Minnesota had a higher percentage of convicts in prison on life sentences than any other state. That didn't make sense, in his judgment. It seemed to him that Minnesota convicts should have the same opportunities as inmates in other states. They should be allowed, after a given period of time, to attempt to convince the parole board that they were ready for release.

On this basis, Berger became a spokesman for Joe Redenbaugh. Word spread, and soon he was besieged with letters from other lifers, some written almost illegibly, some prepared with the precise dignity of a jailhouse lawyer, and all of them pleading for his personal intervention.

Whatever the merits of each individual case—what a man had done, how long he had been incarcerated, what his record was in prison—Ben could empathize with every prisoner's desire to be free and to start a new life. This desire, after all, was what had motivated him to escape from the suffocating atmosphere of Poland at the age of sixteen. Although an innocent victim of anti-Semitism was a far cry from the antisocial creatures who committed criminal acts, the latter—the Joe Redenbaughs of the world—were still human beings, capable of change and worthy of compassion.

Berger was now battling on two fronts. He wanted to win freedom for Redenbaugh, and he wanted to change the law so that other truly rehabilitated lifers had an option besides coming out of prison feet first. But one battle was inextricably bound to the other.

Ben made speeches, wrote letters, and lobbied legislators tirelessly. He knew that the key was Roger Dell, chief justice of the state supreme court, whose words and opinions carried significant legal weight with the legislature. But a determined Ben Berger was a formidable champion of the underdog, and Dell finally conceded the possibility that some convicts deserved another chance. He agreed to support a new law that would allow lifers to appear before the parole board after serving twenty-five years, less time off for good behavior.

Senator Leonard Dickenson of Bemidji, who had agreed to carry the legislative ball for the Minnesota Prisoners Aid Society, called Ben at home to inform him of the extent to which Chief Justice Dell was bending. "I know the change isn't as liberal as you wanted," he conceded. "Do you think we should go ahead?" The question wasn't asked out of mere courtesy. This was Ben's personal crusade; if he didn't approve the change, it could mean they would have to go back to the bargaining table.

But Berger knew when it was time to compromise. "Well, this might be the best we can get," he sighed. "What's your advice?"

"Ben, with Dell's agreement I can put this bill through in a breeze," answered Dickenson. "I may have trouble, though, if you insist on trying to get more. I suggest that you go along with it."

"Okay," said Berger. "Go ahead."

New legislation was enacted by the 1961 legislature. As a result, Joseph Redenbaugh won his opportunity to appeal to the parole board and in 1962, at the age of sixty-four, after serving forty-five years, he walked out of Stillwater Prison.

He stopped in the town of Stillwater to have two beers and called Ben from the bar.

"I'm out," he said quietly.

I know, Joe. That's great."

"I just wanted to thank you, Mr. Berger, for what you did. I appreciate it."

"That's okay. Are you going on to Seattle now?"

"I'm catching the train this afternoon."

"Good luck."

"Thanks," said the freed man.

That was the last that Berger heard from Redenbaugh for eighteen years. He was surprised, expecting to remain in touch at least casually. But obviously Redenbaugh preferred to cut all ties with his painful former life. He changed his name, worked steadily, got married, and later moved to Portland. In 1980, he finally returned to Minnesota for a brief visit.

"I just wanted to let the parole board know that it didn't make a mistake," he told a reporter. "I've kept my nose clean since getting out, haven't been arrested, haven't gotten drunk."

Berger read in the newspaper about Redenbaugh's return and was slightly miffed. He found out where he was staying and telephoned him. "Joe, why didn't you call me when you came back?"

"Sorry. I guess I should have."

The two, now both over eighty years old, met for lunch, and by then Ben's hurt had passed. He had not worked so hard in the other's behalf in order to be paid continual homage. And he had not even done it just for Joe Redenbaugh, but rather for all of the lifers who, without new legislation, would have died in prison.

"I'm satisfied that I did the right thing in helping to get that law changed," says Berger. "Over one hundred rehabilitated people have been freed as a result. That's one hundred or more lives saved in a way, and that's thanks enough for me."

## Chapter Sixteen

When Ben Berger was a young man in Fargo, North Dakota, a baby son was born to one of his former employers in the wholesale fruit business. The child, Arthur Naftalin, grew up to become the first Jewish mayor of the city of Minneapolis, an office he held from 1961 to 1969. The timing was right for Naftalin, whereas Berger burst into civic prominence perhaps a generation too soon.

Several times in the late 1940s and early 1950s, Ben pondered the possibility of running for mayor. He was well known. He had many influential friends. He had the means to build a strong financial base from which to wage a campaign. Although the nomination was not assured, he was certainly an important contender in the ranks of the Republican party, which was not exactly overpopulated with prospects.

But each time he raised his head to sniff the political wind, he decided not to make the race. One can only speculate as to whether Minneapolis would have been ready to elect such a combative, controversial personality as Benjamin Berger, who in addition, and unlike Naftalin, was clearly identified with and involved in Jewish leadership roles. Years later, however, the conditions were right enough for Berger to be twice elected to the Minneapolis Park Board. In the 1969 election, he received the second highest voting total among all candidates running for public office; only the mayoralty winner received more votes.

"I got 59,000 votes," Berger smiled, "and there were probably about six thousand or seven thousand Jewish voters then, so there must have been a few non-Jews willing to vote for me."

He did indeed have broad-based support, which cut across the various religious, racial, and socioeconomic lines of the community. He had earned a reputation as a hard-working philanthropist who cared about the city and its people, gave of himself, took positions according to a firm set of principles, and was willing to "put his money where his mouth was."

\* \* \*

When Berger was a commissioner with the Metropolitan Airports Commission (MAC) in 1974, The Travelers Aid Society encountered financial difficulties in maintaining a booth at Minneapolis-St. Paul International Airport. Through this booth, Travelers Aid provided emergency services to assist the indigent, stranded, lost, handicapped, and ill. Even though Berger and some other commissioners thought this was a commendable and important program, they objected to the society's request to get funding from MAC. They were philosophically opposed to using public money to operate the booth.

Still, Berger believed in the society's work, so at the same meeting in which he pounded the table with his fist and vociferously fought the request, he offered $15,000 of his own money to Travelers Aid if they could raise a similar amount from other private sources. The booth remained open.

Two years later, Berger popped up again in another type of emergency. A series of fires, vandalism, and other incidents had been occurring on the North Side of Minneapolis, where there was a high proportion of blacks. Indications were that the Nazi party and the Ku Klux Klan were responsible for the incidents. To bring peace to the area and stifle a potential outbreak of violence, a suggestion was made to institute temporary neighborhood patrols under conditions sanctioned by the police department. The Minneapolis chapter of the American Red Cross agreed to supply six station wagons for patrolling, and City Council President Louis DeMars then contacted Ben.

Ben's response was to sit down immediately and write a personal check to the city for $5,600 to pay for gas and oil for the patrol vehicles. "The Nazis and Klan should be stopped," he explained, "and I want to help."

Of course it is popular to be involved in such projects. Few people would do anything other than applaud efforts to combat the Nazi party and the Ku Klux Klan. But what has always set Berger apart from the norm is his insistence on standing up and being counted, even in matters of extreme public controversy. "Ben is willing to fight for a cause which may be unpopular, even with his friends," says P. Kenneth Peterson.

Berger, for example, was a member of the parole board when it released the "nylon bandit," William Rankin. Rankin, forty-four, had been convicted of armed robbery three times in twenty-three years, and had been paroled twice before, in 1956 and 1966. The second parole ended when he was caught after participating in a restaurant holdup in which four people were shot.

It was understandable, therefore, that the parole board decision created a furor in the Twin Cities during the normal eight-to-ten-day period between the time a decision is made and the prisoner is actually released. Robert LaBathe, acting police chief in St. Paul, commented succinctly that the parole "stank." Governor Wendell Anderson felt that there was "little reassurance" that Rankin wouldn't return to crime, and he warned, "The safety of Minnesota citizens will be jeopardized by parole at this time." The governor called parole board members to a meeting at his home and asked them to reconsider their decision.

Berger acted as spokesman for the board. At the meeting with the governor and in a newspaper interview, he challenged and rejected the criticism. He pointed out that Rankin had participated in an intensive treatment and counseling program that had changed other previously incorrigible inmates at Stillwater, that he was a very intelligent man, and that he had a job offer.

"The governor is responding to pressure," he said. "The parole was unanimously and very strongly recommended by the prison staff. Rankin has turned over a new leaf and is completely rehabilitated, in my book, and that's what prisons are supposed to do."

The board stuck to its guns, despite the pressure, and Rankin was freed in 1974. Berger is quick to point out that Rankin "to this very day still holds the job he got when he was released, and he has been very helpful to the present parole board."

* * *

Berger also was hit by public criticism in 1977 when he sold his Gopher and Aster theaters in downtown Minneapolis to Edward and Ferris Alexander, brothers who reportedly controlled much of Minnesota' sexually-explicit movie and bookstore industry. The theaters, which have since been torn down, were located on Hennepin Avenue between Sixth and Seventh Streets, in the square block designated for the new City Center development project. City fathers had been resorting to every legal means to get the Alexanders out of downtown Minneapolis. Now they bemoaned the fact that the Gopher and Aster would probably be turned into hardcore sex movie theaters. Also, the city would have to deal with the Alexanders when the time came to acquire the theaters in order to raze them for the City Center.

The *Minneapolis Star* joined in the chorus of condemnation. "Berger complained that Hennepin Avenue is deteriorating and that's why he wanted out," it said in an editorial. "But the city also wants to save Hennepin Avenue. Getting out the way he did can only contribute to further deterioration in that part of town."

To Berger, however, the sale was a straight business deal, pure and simple. "I've been in the theater business for fifty-seven years and I've had about enough of it," he said. "It's time to start cashing in my chips." He added that he had no guilt feelings about selling to the Alexanders. "I don't think that Dayton's Department Store looks up the background of people before selling them furniture, and I don't have to do it, either."

Then he fired one more salvo for good measure. "The same newspaper that said I shouldn't have sold to characters like the Alexanders doesn't mind selling them advertising for their theaters."

Of all the causes championed by Berger, however, and the controversies in which he has entangled himself, none has had more emotion-ridden implications than the abortion issue. In 1977, he contributed $225,000 to Planned Parenthood of Minnesota, which provides abortions during the first three months of pregnancy for poor women who otherwise might wind up, in Berger's words, "going to a back alley butcher." That put Ben in the corner of freedom of choice and in conflict with the powerful right-to-life, anti-abortion movement.

He can accept being in that corner, but he denies the connotation attached to it. In his view, pro-life and pro-choice are oversimplified misnomers. He considers himself both; no one believes in freedom of choice more than Ben Berger, and no one cherishes more the sanctity of life. Ben, for instance, is an implacable opponent of capital punishment. "It's wrong," he feels, "and it's not even a deterrent to crime. States with capital punishment have had more capital crimes percentage-wise than states without such punishment."

Moreover, he is deeply disturbed by "the finality" of execution, inasmuch as he knows of as many as 60 documented cases of people who were convicted of murder and later found to be not guilty. "One of these cases was in Minnesota," he says. "The fellow spent seventeen years in the penitentiary and later it was found that he had been innocent. The legislature then passed a law granting him twenty-five thousand dollars for the mistaken time spent in prison."

Among Berger's most valued possessions is a book presented to him as a gift from Douglas Rigg, who became warden at Stillwater Prison after Leo Utecht, and who also became a fast friend of Ben's. Browsing through an old-book store one day, Rigg discovered a collector's volume, *John Howard and The Prison-World of Europe*, written by Hepworth Dixon and published in 1852.

Howard, an English criminologist born in the 1720s, studied and wrote extensively about man's inhumanity to man, as reflected by the cruelty of the criminal justice system and the sadistic conditions of the prisons of his day. He pointed out the folly of English law, which sentenced people to death for such minimal offenses as pickpocketing; in fact, until the 1830s, England had 200 crimes punishable by hanging. In addition, English law mandated a corporal punishment for felony crimes—a certain amount of lashes, depending on the crime—for everyone sentenced to prison.

This was hardly indicative of a "civilized" society. Moreover, Howard wrote, extreme punishment did not work. Pickpockets, for example, were most often found "working the crowds" that gathered to view hanging of other pickpockets. However, in Berger's view, at least England "realized that it was on the wrong track and eventually did away with capital punishment as well as corporal punishment. Punitive philosophy has been proven wrong," he says, "but America has not yet learned from that which has been proven wrong."

On the inside front cover of the book, Rigg inscribed, "For Ben Berger, Minnesota's 20th Century John Howard."

"To have been equated with John Howard by a man as expert as Douglas Rigg was a supreme honor," says Berger.

\* \* \*

Even though he has not been formally educated in the field of corrections, or in any other field for that matter, Berger learns by listening, observing, and reading. The more he learns the more he is troubled about the rising crime rate and the failure of penal institutions.

"In medicine, they do research to find the causes and cure for a disease," Ben states. "We have to do research to help reduce the incidence of crime."

He has backed his opinions with his money. In 1980, he and his wife set up a $300,000 endowment for the

Mildred and Benjamin Berger Chair of Criminology at Hebrew University in Jerusalem. In 1981, they underwrote—to the tune of $277,000—the costs of an eighteen-month study by the Hubert H. Humphrey Institute of Public Affairs at the University of Minnesota. The study, directed by Professor David Ward, is called the Berger Criminal Violence Project. It was initiated at Berger's suggestion to scientifically investigate cause-and-effect relationships in crime.

"Ben's concerns were shared by the Task Force on Violent Crime established by Attorney General William French Smith," said Harlan Cleveland, director of the Humphrey Institute of Public Affairs. "However, the primary recommendations of the task force did not provide the basis for really effective efforts to prevent the development of criminal careers. We believe that Ben's desire to identify and then publicize factors that produce violent and persistent criminals is a more meaningful contribution to crime control than building more prisons."

In one respect, Berger thinks that his experiences have already given him the answer to the "terrible disease of crime." He has been involved almost continuously since 1952 in various aspects of penal reform and prisoner aid. He was a member of the special governor's Citizens Advisory Committee on Penal Reform for one year and a member of the parole board for eight years. He was also president of the Minnesota Prisoners Aid Society in 1957 and active with that group until the founding of Amicus in 1967, at which point he became president of Amicus.

"During all that time," he says, "I have interviewed several thousand convicts. Eighty percent of the crime in America is committed by children between the ages of ten and eighteen. But these children weren't born anti-social. Circumstances made them that way."

From his interviews, he found that most of those crime-bent children were unwanted. They came from broken families, very often were born to women out of wedlock, and frequently were the sons and daughters of prostitutes. Berger contends that in some cases the problem is aggravated by the Aid to Dependent Children system. "There are many hundreds of thousands of unwed mothers in the United States who in a sense are married to Uncle Sam," he says. "They receive ADC payments while giving birth to four or five or six children by four or five or six different fathers. A great deal of crime is committed by kids who come out of this kind of environment."

So Berger, who talks in absolutes anyway, doesn't mince any words in coming to a conclusion about abortion. "Most pro-life people don't realize it, but they are also pro-crime and pro-prostitution."

For many, that's an incendiary claim. To others, it might seem an overstatement. "There are strong feelings that an unwanted child is headed either for prison or the welfare rolls," mildly concedes P. Kenneth Peterson, "although you could get a pretty good debate about it."

Yet there are those who are equally convinced that Ben is just "telling it like it is," and that his contribution to Planned Parenthood showed enlightened wisdom. One such person is James Otis, a former justice of the Minnesota Supreme Court.

"I would say that ninety percent of the crimes of violence—assault, rapes, murders—come from those who are the result of totally aimless conception," says Justice Otis. "We must recognize and face up to the fact that so many hostile acts are from people who are striking back against the world that has rejected them since the day of their birth, people neglected since birth, those born out of casual alliances, those born to teenagers."

Berger is especially concerned about babies born to girls as young as thirteen or fourteen years old. He contends that these mothers are not able to care for their children, and that the right to abort must be granted to "poor kids" as well as to the wealthy. Without contributions such as his, to organizations such as Planned Parenthood, he sees the poor being turned away and forced to bear children "who will take their revenge on society." Thus he believes that abortion in essence saves lives, adding that in many instances the product of an "aimless conception" agrees. "Many of the inmates I talked to, the murderers and the rapists, would have rather been aborted than put other people and themselves through such suffering," he says.

It would be stretching a point to say that Ben has personally suffered as much as have some of the Stillwater prisoners—not in his darkest days in Poland, or aboard ship to America, or in learning the ways of the capitalist in North Dakota, or even in watching painfully from afar as the Holocaust swept away the family he left behind. Nevertheless, experience has given him a deep appreciation of what it means to suffer. Although Ben does not tend to be outwardly emotional, he is fully capable of understanding another's feelings.

Perhaps, as Judge Riley says, it is true that Ben would not be a desirable volunteer for Amicus. He has not known failure in the same way as the convict who strikes back against society. But he has vivid insight into the convict's despair. On one of his frequent trips abroad, he was deeply affected by a visit to Devil's Island. He inspected the sites where inmates had been chained. He stood at the point where their bodies were thrown to the sharks—for when a prisoner died, he could not be buried in the cemetery. And Ben silently cursed the qualities in human beings that make such acts possible.

\* \* \*

Conversely, Ben can inwardly feel the exhilaration of a people struggling, and succeeding, against great odds. One of Ben and Midge Berger's most poignant memories is of the time they went aboard the Israeli ship, *Kedmah*. It was in 1949, and the ship was bringing immigrants from Marseilles to Haifa. While waiting several days for the *Kedmah* to leave, the Bergers ran into a United Jewish Appeal mission also bound for Israel. They attended a luncheon with the mission and, as they were eating, a familiar figure loomed over their table. It was Chicago newspaper columnist Irv Kupcinet, who had gone to the University of North Dakota more than twenty years earlier. He had been a member of Tau Delta Phi, the Jewish fraternity, which had made Ben an honorary member, and he recognized and remembered Ben as a benefactor of many Jewish students.

"We're flying over to Israel tomorrow, Bennie," said Kupcinet. "Are you and Midge joining us?"

"No," Berger replied. "We want to go by ship with the *olim*."

Temporarily, the Bergers were to regret their decision, for a horrendous five-day trip ensued. There was a violent storm, and the *Kedmah* was not the stately *Queen Mary*, on which they had sailed to Europe in 1937. This ship pitched and rolled to such an extent that people could barely stand up, let alone eat. Many passengers, Midge included, couldn't even get out of their bunks.

At least the Bergers were in one of the boat's two private rooms with bath—the captain had the other. But after the seas calmed, they found to their surprise that they had no running water.

"When we discovered why, though, we didn't complain," says Midge. "The reason was that all of the refugees had used the water to wash the pitifully few garments they had. They wanted to be wearing clean clothes when they got to Israel to make a fresh start in their lives."

There were 410 refugees aboard, most of whom were death camp survivors. Ben had an opportunity to talk to some of them. They told about getting up each morning and wondering if they were going to live through the day. They didn't know how they had done it, how they happened to be fortunate enough to survive and to be on this ship. It was a miracle, they said.

As the port of Haifa appeared ahead, the *olim* gathered on deck. They sang, waved, cried, and laughed. When the ship docked and the gangplank was lowered, they disembarked as if seeing a mirage, and many of them literally kissed the ground of Israel. Midge describes it as a "tremendously exciting, moving, and significant moment." And to Ben, it was also a reminder that most European Jews, including his parents and sisters, had not survived. No one would ever have to lecture him on how precious life and freedom were, whether for his Jewish brethren from Europe, or a convict paroled from Stillwater Prison, or a pregnant girl seeking an abortion.

\* \* \*

Had Berger ever become mayor of Minneapolis, his would have been an activist administration, replete with ideas and arguments. He would have gotten jobs done, although probably biting off more than he could chew. Most certainly he would have offended some citizens with his brashness and bluntness, but he also would have spread a wide measure of joy as well.

Berger sets off sparks, no matter what he tries. Either he makes things happen, or things happen to him, or both. His misadventures are legend among his friends. Anecdotes about him abound, and he has been blessed with the innate capacity to cheerily dismiss life's foibles.

Many years ago, he placed a $200 bet in New York on the first Joe Louis-Max Schmeling heavyweight fight. Louis was favored at seven to one—few experts gave Schmeling a chance. But Berger, who was always known as a lucky gambler, was one of the few. He bet on Schmeling because it was a good long shot and he never minded bucking the odds. Schmeling won. After the fight when Berger went to collect his $1,400, the bookmaker had departed for parts unknown. It could only have happened to Bennie, his friends nodded.

Berger also is renowned, in a way, for his golf game. He has been playing for about fifty years and has never broken 100. He kids himself about it. "I am the most consistent golfer in the world," he remarks. "When I joined Oak Ridge Country Club in 1930, I had a thirty-six handicap, and I still have that same handicap today."

In the early 1950s, he was once a partner with Sam Snead in a pro-am celebrity tournament at Oak Ridge. The *Minneapolis Star's* Jim Klobuchar described in a column how Ben "stepped to the tee, waggled pudgily, and swung." As Snead watched aghast, the ball sputtered ten feet *behind* the tee, continued into a tree, and expired at the foot of Snead's caddie, forty yards away.

"Surely this has got to be a jest," Klobuchar quoted Snead as observing. "Either that or this man is one of the best trick shots I have ever seen."

Assured by an Oak Ridge regular that this was simply Ben Berger in action, the "clearly shaken" Snead sent his first shot into a lake, never really recovered, and hasn't played a round at Oak Ridge since.

Even when standing harmlessly on the sidelines, Berger somehow generates controversy. While in Sydney, Australia in 1968, he saw a fountain designed by Australian sculptor Robert Woodward. He fell in love with it, and later commissioned construction of a replica to donate to his beloved Minneapolis. But when the fountain was finally ready for installation in 1973, a storm broke over where to put it. The location chosen originally, across from the Guthrie Theater and Walker Art Center, had to be abandoned because of protests from the institutions and neighborhood groups. They felt that the design, with water shooting through a circular arrangement of spines to form a spray about seventeen feet in diameter, did not artistically suit the area.

The Park and Recreation Board, whose assignment it was to find a spot for the fountain, then ran into similar protests from other groups about other locations. Berger, who was a member of the board, deliberately refrained from participating in any of the discussions. He feared that someone would accuse him of dictating a location.

"I'm just an innocent bystander," he said plaintively. "All I wanted to do was give a fountain to the city. I never dreamed that there would be any objections. I don't care where it goes, but I would like it to go somewhere while I'm still alive."

After many months of bickering, Loring Park on the outskirts of downtown was selected as the site for the "Berger Fountain," which cost Ben $242,000 by the time it was finally installed in 1975. Despite fears of some area residents that "this will overwhelm and spoil the natural beauty of Loring Park and be a tragic environmental blight," the structure has done nothing of the kind. Rather, it has become an accepted and admired part of the scenery, a focal point for children at play, for their relaxed parents, for joggers, for strollers, for the community.

It was a tribute from a man to his city, but it has also come to represent a reason for the city and its citizens to pay tribute to the man. As a letter to the *Minneapolis Star* stated, "Berger is the epitome of a young-thinking free soul. It would be a pleasure to know him and work with him. Abraham Lincoln once said, 'I like to see a man live so that his place will be proud of him.' Minneapolis is such a place. Benjamin Berger is such a man."

# Chapter Seventeen

*I've been fortunate in my life, and I've tried to share my good fortune. Naturally you take care of your family first. My son, Bobby (his real name is Lawrence), from my first marriage, spent much of his growing-up years living with us, with Midge and me, and I've tried to help him as much as I could. Together we had majority ownership of the ABC Network television station in Honolulu, Hawaii, KHVH, for about ten years, until selling out in 1975. He lives in Honolulu and owns radio stations there and on Samoa and Guam. He also owns a television station on Guam. Midge and I are proud of him, his wife, Jackie, and our grandchildren, Robert and William. They were all in Minneapolis when International B'nai B'rith honored us in 1980.*

*I tried to help my brothers, too, and their families. One of my nephews, Isaac Berger, lived with us and went to high school here and to the University of Minnesota. I got him a job and he has gone on to do very well on his own as an executive with a big company.*

I think all this is fine. But there's more to life than just meeting responsibilities to yourself or your family. I've always felt an obligation to give back something to the country that has made so much possible for me, the country that gave me my freedom and the opportunity to succeed. Giving back to the country means giving back to the people who need your help, people who can't help themselves. Doing that makes the country stronger.

There's nothing I wouldn't do for America. I'm not ashamed to be so patriotic. I've received hundreds of plaques and citations and honors, but I'm especially proud of papers that represent my service to and my feelings about America: my citizenship papers, my honorable discharge from the United States Army, my honorable discharge from the National Guard when I was in Fargo, the recognition I have received from veterans organizations. In 1979, I was elected commander of the Peterson American Legion Post in Minneapolis. They knew that at this stage of my life I wasn't going to be an active commander, but this was their way of honoring me. But I'm the one who should be honoring them.

I'm not blind about this country. I know we have problems. I'm very concerned about our crime rate, the worst in the world—for every 100,000 people, we have 224 behind bars. The second worst rate is in Canada, 98 out of 100,000. The Scandinavian countries have only 37, and the Netherlands has the lowest—25 per 100,000.

We've got to do something to turn the tide around. Crime in America has increased by 1000 percent since 1936. In this decade, we will be spending a billion dollars to build prisons. We've got to put our brains to work solving the problem of crime, the disease of crime, a manmade disease. We must get away from the punitive philosophy—as represented, for example, by determinate sentencing laws. We must work on methods of rehabilitation and develop plans to release every inmate who is completely rehabilitated. This will give inmates an 'incentive' to be rehabilitated. Of course I don't want criminals walking the streets. As a matter of fact, I would like to see our jury system changed so that a verdict can be reached by ten of the twelve jurors. I think that prosecuting attorneys sometimes plea bargain when they shouldn't, because they are afraid that they won't be able to get a unanimous verdict and a murderer might be put out on the street again. My way, one or two jurors will not be able to hang up a case. I think this will make for a better correctional system, assuming that we can start getting to the causes of crime in the first place and then start an intelligent program of rehabilitation.

We can improve our system of government, too. Not that it isn't a thousand times better than any other system, and I've studied many of them. One system I know plenty about is the communist system. I've been to Russia five times and to every satellite country several times, and the communist system is so rotten that I predict it will break up before the end of the century.

The very reason for the original Russian Revolution was to knock out the people who had been enjoying the fruits of slave labor. But today there is just as much aristocracy in Russia as there was before the Revolution. The workers are still slaves, and they will be less and less willing to fight for Russia. Also, the Soviet Union is surrounded by satellite countries that are too nationalistic to remain forever in the Russian camp. I predict that when the Russian leaders of today, who are in their sixties and seventies, start dying off, Russia will begin losing its satellite countries and start turning toward a socialist rather than a communist system.

But the fact that Russia has troubles doesn't mean that our system of government can't be better. For example, I don't like the way that a person just elected to office starts running for reelection the next day. I think that the next day he should be concerned about doing a job in the term he has been elected to. I would like to see one six-year term for president, a maximum of two terms for the Senate, and also some sort of maximum for the House. I hope something like that will happen someday to improve our political system.

I am concerned and mad about anti-Semitism, too. This hatred against Jews did not start right after Christ. When the Roman Empire controlled most of Europe for the first five hundred years A.D., they harassed Christians, not Jews. In the next five hundred years, Europe was controlled by the Ottoman Empire. These people were Semites and considered Jews their cousins, so there was no anti-Semitism during that period, either.

It was only in the last one thousand years, when European countries turned Christian, that troubles began for the Jews. These countries needed a scapegoat. Jews became the scapegoat. People were uneducated, and when the church told them that the Jews had killed Christ, and that Jews were to blame for their problems, they believed it. In Germany, for example, they blamed Jews for crop failures.

That kind of thinking has led to torture and death for millions of Jews over the centuries. Christians burned "nonbelievers" at the stake for the "crime" of being born Jewish and for refusing to convert. If they did convert, suddenly they became "respectable." Anti-Semitism finally brought about the massacres and pogroms that led to the Holocaust.

The same kind of thinking has devastated other peoples, too. Discrimination, like crime, is a man-made disease and takes more lives than natural diseases. I think that discrimination contributed to the war between Russia and

Japan in 1905, to the massacre shortly after of a million and a half Armenians by Turkey, and to both World Wars. In my opinion, there have been over 100 million murders in this century because of discrimination.

As angry as I am about the past, however, I am hopeful about the future. Times are changing. This country, for instance, is not as anti-Semitic today as it was when I got here, or in the 1930s. I know that there still are plenty of ignorant and uneduated people who hate Jews. But the intelligent Christian clergyman isn't anti-Semitic, nor are the people who are learned and familiar with the Old and New Testaments. No intelligent, educated Christian could possibly be anti-Semitic, because so many thousands of Jews embraced the teachings of Christ. The first fifty bishops in history were circumcised Jews. If there hadn't been an Old Testament, there would never have been a New Testament, and if there hadn't been a Jewish religion, there would never have been a Christian religion.

Early in this century, some Christian leaders in this country realized that something had to be done to promote better understanding between Christians and Jews. This resulted in establishment of the National Conference of Christians and Jews (NCCJ). I am proud to have been an NCCJ board member in Minnesota for close to forty years. I believe this organization has been—and will continue to be—an inspiration for other organizations and individuals to do away with anti-Semitism or "anti" anything else.

After the Holocaust, the attitude of the Christian hierarchy toward Jews changed even more. Christian leaders started to truly recognize the wrongs that have been done to the Jews for so many years. I think that they will ask our forgiveness someday. I think that before the turn of the century, the Christian hierarchy will publicly apologize to the Jewish people for a thousand years of suffering, and that on a given Sunday the bells will chime in churches throughout the world, proclaiming a new era of brotherhood.

This can happen because, if discrimination is a disease made by man, then man can un-make it. I suggest that all religions in all places of worship preach against the disease of discrimination, which has caused so many murders for so many hundreds of years. The media, particularly television, should also be utilized in a world-wide drive against this disease.

It will be a beautiful day when we can finally eliminate intolerance and bitterness among peoples. The sooner we get rid of prejudice and hatred, the sooner people will learn to live together as equals, in harmony and in peace.

I have a great feeling that this day will come, and I am optimistic that we can show the way in America. I believe in America. I know what we've done, and I know what we can do, especially if the "haves" recognize their obligations to the "have-nots." I have tried to recognize mine, and I'm proud of the contributions I have made and will continue making as long as I live.

It's my way of saying, "Thank You, America," for all you have given me.

Partial Listing of Benjamin N. Berger Memorabilia

1. Citation from Variety Clubs International "in recognition of outstanding service and dedication to Variety in helping underprivileged and handicapped children."
2. "Authentic barbed wire" from the Iron Curtain, awarded by the Heritage Foundation "in recognition of your distinguished aid to Crusade for Freedom."
3. Humanitarian Award for 1978 from Planned Parenthood.
4. Certificate of Appreciation from President Nixon for serving as a member of the United Service Organization, 1972.
5. Invitation from President Eisenhower and admission card to Northwest Gate of the White House. June 29, 1954.
6. Plaque from Jewish National Fund, given to Ben and Mildred Berger "for their untiring, unlimited, and unselfish dedication to the betterment of their community, their country, the State of Israel, and the Jewish National Fund project in Israel."
7. Presentation from the Minneapolis Park and Recreation Board, "in grateful appreciation for donation of the Berger Fountain to the citizens of Minneapolis."
8. B'nai B'rith Services Appeal plaque.
9. Annual International B'nai B'rith Humanitarian Award, 1980.
10. Certificate, Ben Berger Forest in Israel, Jewish National Fund.
11. Engraved memento, with players signatures, from the Minneapolis Lakers, world champions, "in grateful appreciation to Benjamin N. Berger for guidance and support through these many years."

12. Certificate of appreciation for "devoted service and leadership on behalf of United Jewish Appeal."
13. Bonds for Israel "Award of Honor" for bond sales.
14. Plaque from Histadrut "for loyal and distinguished service to the pioneering builders of Israel."
15. From the Variety Club of the Northwest, a plaque in recognition "of outstanding service, unstinting devotion of time and energies as Chief Barker."
16. Plaque from Amicus, presented September 14, 1974 by Elliott Richardson on behalf of a grateful community.
17. Certificate of appreciation, American Bicentennial Park in Israel.
18. Good Neighbor Award, WCCO Radio.
19. Citation for endowment, Mildred and Benjamin Berger Chair of Criminology, Hebrew University.
20. Proclamation from Minneapolis Mayor Albert Hofstede, proclaiming Benjamin Berger Day, August 24, 1975.

Past and Present Activities and Affiliations
(Partial Listing)

1. President, Berger Amusement Company.
2. Owner, Schiek's Cafe.
3. President, Independent Theatre Owners for Minnesota, North Dakota, and South Dakota.
4. President, Minneapolis Lakers basketball team.
5. President, Minneapolis Millers hockey club.
6. One of three signers to secure North Dakota charter for Veterans of Foreign Wars.
7. Treasurer of Veterans of Foreign Wars post, Fargo, North Dakota.

# Thank You, America 223

8. President, B'nai B'rith, Grand Forks, North Dakota.
9. Vice Commander, American Legion, Grand Forks, North Dakota.
10. Member, National USO board.
11. Representative for U.S. Government at first Berlin Film Festival.
12. State chairman, Radio Free Europe.
13. Vice chairman, Governor Anderson's Citizens Advisory Committee on Penal Reform.
14. Chairman, Mayor's Citizens Committee of Minneapolis Workhouse.
15. President, Minnesota Prisoners Aid Society.
16. President (and presently chairman of the board) of Amicus.
17. Member, Minnesota Corrections Authority (the state parole board).
18. Part owner of the ABC television station, KHVH, in Honolulu.
19. Chief Barker (President) Variety Club of the Northwest.
20. Member of the board, Temple Israel.
21. Chairman to raise $250,000 for Temple Israel's new Hebrew School building.
22. First state chairman, Bonds for Israel.
23. President, Minnesota Jewish National Fund.
24. President, Minneapolis Histadrut.
25. President, Minneapolis Zionist Organization.
26. Member of the board, National Conference of Christians and Jews.
27. Commander, American Legion, Peterson Post, Minneapolis.
28. Deputy Sheriff of Hennepin County.
29. Commencement speaker, Lea College, Albert Lea, Minnesota.

30. Member, Governor's Council on Health, Welfare, and Rehabilitation.
31. Member, Minneapolis Aquatennial board.
32. Member, Metropolitan Airports Commission, Minneapolis-St. Paul.
33. Member, Minneapolis Park Board.